FORTRESS • 65

THE FORTS OF JUDAEA 168 BC–AD 73

From the Maccabees to the Fall of Masada

SAMUEL ROCCA

ILLUSTRATED BY ADAM HOOK

Series editors Marcus Cowper and Nikolai Bogdanovic

First published in Great Britain in 2008 by Osprey Publishing,
Midland House, West Way, Botley, Oxford OX2 0PH, United Kingdom
443 Park Avenue South, New York, NY 10016, USA
Email: info@ospreypublishing.com

A CIP catalogue record for this book is available from the British Library.

ISBN-13 978 1 84603 171 7

Editorial by Ilios Publishing, Oxford, UK (www.iliospublishing.com)
Page layout by Ken Vail Graphic Design, Cambridge, UK (kvgd.com)
Cartography: Map Studio Ltd, Romsey, UK
Typeset in Sabon and Myriad Pro
Index by Alan Thatcher
Originated by PDQ Digital Media Imaging, UK
Printed and bound in China through Bookbuilders

07 08 09 10 11   10 9 8 7 6 5 4 3 2 1

FOR A CATALOGUE OF ALL BOOKS PUBLISHED BY OSPREY MILITARY
AND AVIATION PLEASE CONTACT:

NORTH AMERICA
Osprey Direct, c/o Random House Distribution Center, 400 Hahn Road,
Westminster, MD 21157
Email: info@ospreydirect.com

ALL OTHER REGIONS
Osprey Direct UK, PO Box 140, Wellingborough,
Northants, NN8 2FA, UK
Email: info@ospreydirect.co.uk

www.ospreypublishing.com

DEDICATION

This book is dedicated to the memory of Fausto Rocca, Genio, Regio
Esercito 1915–18, 1943–45 and to the memory of Boris Carmi, 524 Coy,
RE 1941–46.

ACKNOWLEDGEMENTS

This book had been made possible through the help of Dr Moti Aviam
(Institute of Galilean Archaeology, University of Rochester); the late
Professor Yizhar Hirschfeld (The Hebrew University of Jerusalem), Holyland
Hotel – Jerusalem; Dr Danny Syon (Gamla excavations); the Israel Nature
and Parks Authority; Dalit Weinblatt–Krausz, and Photodoron.

ARTIST'S NOTE

Readers may care to note that the original paintings from which the
colour plates in this book were prepared are available for private sale.
All reproduction copyright whatsoever is retained by the Publishers.
All enquiries should be addressed to:

Scorpio Gallery, PO Box 475, Hailsham, East Sussex, UK

The Publishers regret that they can enter into no correspondence upon
this matter.

THE FORTRESS STUDY GROUP (FSG)

The object of the FSG is to advance the education of the public in the study
of all aspects of fortifications and their armaments, especially works
constructed to mount or resist artillery. The FSG holds an annual
conference in September over a long weekend with visits and evening
lectures, an annual tour abroad lasting about eight days, and an annual
Members' Day.

The FSG journal *FORT* is published annually, and its newsletter *Casemate*
is published three times a year. Membership is international. For further
details, please contact:

The Secretary, c/o 6 Lanark Place, London W9 1BS, UK

THE WOODLAND TRUST

Osprey Publishing are supporting the Woodland Trust, the UK's leading
woodland conservation charity, by funding the dedication of trees.

CONTENTS

THE FORTS OF JUDAEA 168 BC–AD 73 FROM THE MACCABEES TO THE FALL OF MASADA

INTRODUCTION

The period from 168 BC until AD 73 (known as the Second Temple period) was an important one in the history of the Jewish people, and is often considered a golden age where the Jews achieved complete political independence. The fortifications erected by the Hasmonaean and the Herodian rulers that held sway during this period fulfilled a variety of important tasks. First and foremost was the defence of the areas in which they were located. In times of peace, some controlled the main highways of the kingdom, such as the fortresses of Hyrcania, Alexandrium and Masada, their small garrisons keeping the constant threat of brigands and outlaws away. The royal palaces of the Hasmonaeans and Herod, which lay at the very centre of power, were protected by chains of fortresses around them. Good examples are provided by the Antonia fortress and the Citadel towers in Jerusalem, which protected Herod's palace and the Temple; and the fortress of Cyprus, which protected Herod's palaces at Jericho. Other fortresses, such as Herodium, acted as regional capitals. In addition, some fortresses served as prisons for political prisoners, the most famous being Herod's sons Alexander and Aristobulus who were jailed in Sebaste, and John the Baptist, who was a prisoner of Antipas in the fortress of Machaerous. Last but not least, these fortresses were statements of the power of the Hasmoneans and Herodian rulers of Judaea.

Historical background

After the destruction of the First Temple (erected by King Solomon) in 586 BC, most of the Judaeans were exiled to Babylonia. However, in 549 BC Cyrus, the Achaemenid ruler of the Medes and the Persians, conquered Babylonia. He gave the Jews permission to return to Judaea and to rebuild the temple. The exiles did so and built the Second Temple, and in the process created a small theocratic state under the leadership of the high priest.

However, Judaea subsequently fell under the control of Alexander the Great, the Ptolemies and the Seleucids. The Jews were allowed freedom of worship until the Seleucid ruler Antiochus IV began a programme of forced Hellenization, obliging the Jews to discard the Torah, their ancestral law, and forbidding circumcision. A Jewish rebellion against the Seleucid overlords was led by Judah Maccabaeus. After several victorious battles, the Jews achieved political independence under the leadership of the Hasmonaean dynasty (the descendants of Judah Maccabaeus), and Hasmonaean Judaea became a small regional power. The Maccabean leaders cleverly exploited the civil war in and disintegration of the decaying Seleucid state, at times siding with the legitimate rulers and on other occasions with the various usurpers. Thus from rebel leaders the Maccabees were recognized by the Seleucid ruler as High Priest, as the spiritual leaders of the Jews, and ethnarch, as the secular rulers of Judaea. Nevertheless, at least until the rule of Simon the Hasmonaean, Judaea remained a *de jure* vassal of the Seleucid kingdom, despite securing an alliance with faraway Republican Rome.

Under the leadership of John Hyrcanus, son of Simon, the small Hasmonaean state conquered the neighbouring regions of Idumaea, Samaria and Galilee, and secured the harbour of Joppa, the gateway to the Mediterranean. John Hyrcanus erected various fortifications to defend Judaea proper, the core of the kingdom. In Jerusalem he built the First Wall, and in the Judaean desert he erected the fortifications at Hyrcania that controlled the King's Highway.

In the Late Hellenistic period Alexander Jannaeus made Hasmonean Judaea a first-rate power. He defeated the Ptolemaic ruler Ptolemy X Latyrus, the Seleucid kings Demetrius III Eucareus and Antiochus XII, and the neighbouring Nabataeans. Alexander Jannaeus also annexed most of the coastal strip of the land of Israel and vast areas of the Transjordan region. However, the price of success was high, and it resulted in a long civil war with his Jewish subjects, led by the Pharisees. Still, in 76 BC, Alexander Jannaeus was able to leave to his wife, Queen Salome Alexandra, a state that touched the borders of the legendary kingdom of David and Solomon.

After ten years of peace, in 66 BC tensions between the two sons of Alexander Jannaeus and Salome Alexandra, Hyrcanus II and Aristobulus II, erupted into civil war. Hyrcanus II was supported by Antipater the Idumaean and the Pharisees, while Aristobulus was supported by the Sadducees. The civil war ended in 63 BC when Pompey, having annexed Seleucid Syria, sided himself with Hyrcanus II, besieged Aristobulus II in Jerusalem, stormed the city, and brought Aristobulus to Rome in chains.

Pompey, and later Gabinius, the Roman governor of Syria, redrew the map of the region between 63 and 57 BC. The Hasmonaean kingdom of Judaea was cut off from the coastal region, and Decapolis, the northern part of the Transjordanian region, whose population was predominantly Greek and was traditionally hostile to the Hasmonaeans. Hyrcanus II lost the title of king (although he retained the title of high priest). However, in the civil war between Pompey and Julius Caesar, Hyrcanus II (guided by his influential counsellor Antipater) gave help to the latter in his Alexandrian war. Caesar rewarded him by giving back part of the lost territories and making Hyrcanus II 'ethnarches' or secular ruler of Judaea.

The civil war between the assassins of Julius Caesar, Brutus and Cassius and Antony and the young Caesar Octavian held plentiful consequences for Hasmonaean Judaea. Antipater, the powerful counsellor of Hyrcanus II, was murdered by rivals. Moreover in 40 BC the Parthians, sensing Rome's weakness, invaded Syria and Judaea. With them came the young Antigonus, the son of the deposed Aristobulus II. The Parthians appointed him king and high priest of Judaea. Antigonus took his revenge on the elderly Hyrcanus II, but the young Herod, son of Antipater, escaped to Rome. Whilst there, Herod convinced Antony and Octavian to have the Senate crown him King of Judaea. One year later, Herod was back in Judaea. By then the Parthians had retreated over the border, leaving Antigonus to his fate. However, it took Herod three years

(until 37 BC) to conquer his kingdom. Herod was backed by most of the Jews, who had grown tired of Antigonus's tyranny, and by a Roman army under the command of Sosius. Herod married the beautiful Mariamne, the granddaughter of Hyrcanus II, adding the prestige of the Hasmonaean family to his pedigree. When Herod finally entered Jerusalem in 37 BC, Antigonus was sent to Antony, who had him beheaded.

The early years of King Herod's rule were not easy. His main enemy was no less than Cleopatra, Queen of Egypt. In 32 BC, while Antony and Cleopatra were fighting against Octavian at Actium, Herod was locked in combat with the Nabataeans as well as a Ptolemaic army, sent against him by Cleopatra, even though he was an ally of Antony's. These distractions prevented Herod from sending reinforcements to Antony in his struggle with Octavian. For this reason, when Octavian received Herod at Rhodes in 30 BC, Herod was reconfirmed as King of Judaea. Moreover, Octavian returned to Herod all the territories given by Antony to Cleopatra. In the ensuing years, Augustus (formerly Octavian) granted Herod Trachonitis, Batanaea and Auranitis (23–22 BC), and Ituraea (20 BC). In exchange, in 25 BC Herod sent a contingent to assist Aelius Gallus, the governor of Egypt, in his disastrous Arabian campaign, and in 15 BC his fleet assisted Agrippa in his campaigns in the Cimmerian Bosphorus.

Herod was a great builder. He constructed a series of royal palaces in every corner of the kingdom, in addition to founding the two Greek cities of Sebaste and Caesarea Maritima, the latter equipped with a modern harbour. In Jerusalem he rebuilt the Temple, erected a new wall (the Second Wall), and built the multi-storey towers above his palace and the Antonia fortress to guard the huge Temple Mount. Herod also erected the tetrapyrgion of Herodium, as well as fortifying Masada. In addition, the Hasmonaean Desert fortresses of Hyrcania, Alexandrium and Machaerous were renovated.

Herod's final years were unhappy ones. A series of petty family squabbles (Herod had no fewer than nine wives and thus many potential heirs) brought him to execute his beautiful wife Mariamne, and later his two sons by her, Alexander and Aristobulus (a few days before Herod's death, his son Antipater by his first wife Doris was also executed). It is no surprise to learn that Augustus joked that it was better to be a pig than a son of the Jewish king. Moreover, in 9 BC the Second Nabataean War brought the wrath of Augustus down on Herod. Although it was clear that Herod was not responsible for starting the war, which had been declared without Augustus's permission (the main instigator being the Nabataean vizier Syllaeus), Herod suffered a breakdown. When he died in 4 BC,

suffering from mental illness, Herod's kingdom was divided between his three sons Archelaus, Antipas and Philip. Archelaus, appointed to the role of ethnarch by Augustus, received Judaea, Samaria and Idumaea. Archelaus's brothers were granted the lesser title of tetrarch. Antipas received Galilee and Peraea, while Philip received the northern territories around the Golan region.

Archelaus proved to be a poor ruler. As early as 4 BC, the population of Judaea rebelled against his rule. In AD 6, after ten years of unhappy rule, he was dismissed by Augustus and sent into exile in Gaul. His territories were administered by a Roman governor, a *praefectus* of equestrian rank; the latter was responsible to the Roman governor of Syria, who was of superior senatorial rank. Most of the subsequent governors carried out their duties successfully. The only exception was the cruel and corrupt Pontius Pilatus, who ruled Judaea between AD 26 and 36.

TOP LEFT
A coin of Agrippa I (AD 41–44), minted probably in AD 42/43 at Caesarea Maritima. The obverse depicts the head of Agrippa, with the Tyche of Caesarea Maritima, symbol of the city, on the reverse. (Private collection)

TOP RIGHT
A coin issued by Felix (AD 52–59), procurator of Judaea during the reign of Claudius, minted in AD 54. The obverse depicts a Celtic crossed shield, to celebrate the Claudian conquest of Britannia, while the reverse depicts the palm tree, symbol of Judaea. (Private collection)

Archelaus's brothers fared better. Philip ruled his territories until AD 33. Antipas, who ruled until AD 39, urbanized his kingdom, continuing in Herod's footsteps. He founded the city of Tiberias, named in honour of the Roman emperor Tiberius. Judaea reverted to independent status under the rule of Agrippa I, grandson of Herod and Mariamne the Hasmonaean. The young Agrippa had been educated at the imperial court in Rome, where he became friends with the future emperors Caligula and Claudius. Agrippa was well rewarded by his imperial friends. In AD 33 Caligula granted him the territories belonging to Philip, following the latter's death, and in AD 39 he received the territories of Antipas on his exile to southern Gaul. Claudius also gave Agrippa Judaea itself, the core of the kingdom.

Agrippa ruled for three peaceful years from AD 41 to 44. Among his achievements was the erection of the Third Wall of Jerusalem. On his death Claudius annexed the whole kingdom, and appointed an equestrian governor, with the rank of procurator. Most of the subsequent governors were characterized by cruelty and corruption, and tensions between the Jews and the Romans rose. The priestly aristocracy, who although siding with the Romans tried to protect their subjects from Roman oppression, were viewed as collaborators by most of the Jews. On the other side, the extremist movements of the Zealots and the Sicarii gained a foothold among the population.

The Jewish-Roman War
In AD 66 Gessius Florus, the governor of Judaea, brought the province to rebellion by taking money from the coffers of the Temple, outraging the population. Gessius was forced to flee to Caesarea Maritima. Meanwhile, in Jerusalem a government composed of moderate leaders began to organize the war effort against the might of Rome, although their efforts were hampered by the extremist Zealot and Sicarii groups, who wished to take over leadership. Cestius Gallus, the governor of Syria, launched an unsuccessful attack against Jerusalem, and during the retreat of his army the Jews inflicted a defeat on him at Beth Horon. This victory brought about a rebellion inside the kingdom of Agrippa II, the son of Agrippa I, which consisted of most of Galilee and the Golan region.

In Jerusalem a new government was formed, composed mainly of Sadducees, which set about organizing the defence of Judaea in preparation for the Roman onslaught. Among the military commanders was the young

This silver sheqel dates from the time of the First Revolt. The obverse depicts the Chalice of the Omer, used in the Temple ceremonies, while the reverse shows a branch bearing three pomegranates. The coin was minted in AD 69–70. (Private collection)

This silver denarius minted by Titus celebrates 'Judaea Capta' and depicts the head of the Roman emperor on the obverse. The reverse depicts a Roman soldier standing near a palm tree, the symbol of Judaea; under the tree is a forlorn-looking seated Jewess. (Private collection)

aristocratic priest Joseph ben Mattitiyahu – better known as the historian Josephus – who was given the command of Galilee. Agrippa II, however, remained faithful to the Romans. The Roman emperor Nero was notified of the Jewish rebellion during his visit to Greece. He then called on the services of Vespasian, a general who had already distinguished himself during Claudius's conquest of Britannia. In AD 67 Vespasian arrived at Antiochia and organized his army, which included a contingent of Agrippa II's troops. Vespasian was joined at Ptolemais by his son Titus.

The Jews knew that they could not face the Roman army in the open field. As a result, the fighting was principally focused on the siege of cities, fortified villages and fortresses. Vespasian first attacked Galilee. Joseph ben Mattitiyahu (Josephus), the Jewish commander, was soon besieged in the stronghold of Jotapata, which was eventually taken by the Romans; once freed, Josephus became the official historian of the Jewish War. After the fall of Jotapata, the city of Tiberias surrendered to Agrippa II. Meanwhile, following a short siege, Titus took the fortress of Tarichae. From Galilee, Vespasian's army moved to the Golan, to besiege the city-fortress of Gamla; it fell within a few months. The remaining stronghold of Gush Halav surrendered to Titus.

In Jerusalem the loss of Galilee brought civil war between the moderate leaders and the extremist Zealot and Sicarii factions. Having murdered their opponents, the latter began a vicious inter-factional war of their own, which brought Jerusalem to the point of starvation. By the end of AD 67 Vespasian's army had reconquered the Peraea region, Decapolis and most of Judaea. Only Jerusalem and certain fortresses (including Masada and Herodium) withstood the Roman onslaught. However, much of AD 68 and 69 saw little fighting, as

A NEXT PAGE: JERUSALEM IN AD 44

A reconstruction of Jerusalem in AD 44. It should be noted that many of the locations of these sites are controversial, and no definitive plan of Jerusalem during this period exists.

1. Temple Mount	**5.** Antonia fortress	**11.** Second Wall
1a. Outer Court	**6.** Siloam Pool	**12.** Third Wall
1b. Inner Court	**7.** Herod's Palace	**13.** Citadel (including the
2. New City	**8.** Hippodrome	Psephinus, Hyppicus,
3. Lower City	**9.** Theatre	and Mariamne towers)
4. Upper City	**10.** First Wall	

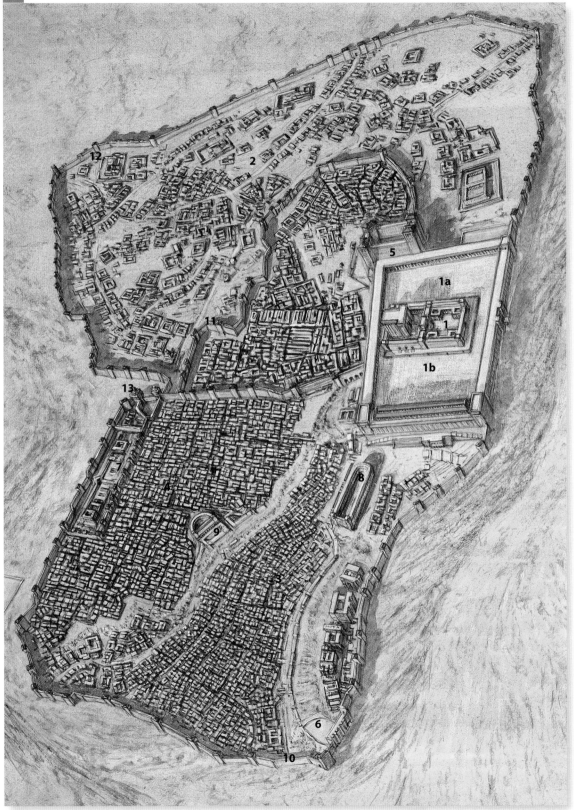

a major civil war had broken out in Rome itself following the suicide of Nero. When Vespasian emerged triumphant as emperor, he appointed his son Titus as military commander of the war in Judaea. The three walls of Jerusalem were successively overcome by the Romans, the Antonia fortress was razed to the ground, and in the subsequent clash the Temple was completely burned down. The main Jewish leaders, Yochanan of Gush Halav and Shimon Bar Giora, were taken prisoner. After the siege of Jerusalem, Titus left Judaea for Rome. In AD 72 Flavius Silva was appointed governor of Judaea. His main undertaking was to reduce the stronghold of Masada, in the hands of Eleazar ben Yair, which still defied the Romans. The last phase of the war witnessed the siege of Masada, in AD 72–73, where the besieged defenders opted to kill themselves rather than to be enslaved by the Romans. The episode not only put an end to the Jewish Revolt, but also to Jewish independence.

The Hasmonaean kingdom *c.* 76 BC

DESIGN AND DEVELOPMENT

Hasmonaean fortifications

In 168 BC, when the Hasmonaeans began their war against the Seleucid overlords of Judaea, the fortifications in the Land of Israel, then part of Coele-Syria, presented a mix of local traditions, inherited from the Iron Age as well as the Hellenistic period. The main types of fortifications faced by the Hasmonaean army were city walls and small fortlets. The city walls of the Greek cities of southern Coele-Syria shared similar features with the Hellenistic fortifications in the eastern Mediterranean, but the small fortlets clearly showed local influences.

Evolution and function

The Hasmonaean fortifications evolved in two basic phases. In the first, from the beginning of the Hasmonaean revolt (168 BC) until the rule of Simon (143–135 BC), the Hasmonaean rulers repaired the existing Ptolemaic and Seleucid fortifications – or rather, their forces destroyed most of the existing fortifications as they were of more use to the Seleucids than to their own small mobile army, which could not spare soldiers for garrison duty. The destruction of the Akra fortification in Jerusalem is a striking example of this policy.

Only under John Hyrcanus I's rule did the Hasmonaeans begin a well-defined programme of fortification building. The main purpose of the Hasmonaean fortifications was to protect Judaea, the core of the kingdom. The newly conquered areas, such as Galilee, Idumaea and Samaria, were not fortified; it seems that the Hasmonaeans used the existing Ptolemaic and Seleucid fortifications in these areas, and settled military colonies. However, in Judaea itself the Hasmonaeans began a massive programme of fortification. John Hyrcanus erected the First Wall of Jerusalem, which encompassed all the residential areas of the city. The Winter Palaces of Jericho were also surrounded by a series of fortifications, whose main purpose was to guard these palaces, the second most important administrative centre after Jerusalem. The Hasmonaeans erected various forts, among them Hyrcania in the Desert of Judaea, Alexandrium on the border with Samaria, and Machaerous in Peraea (Transjordan). Clearly the purpose of these fortifications was neither defence nor the control of the main roads, as these fortifications were far removed from urban centres as well as highways. The main purpose of these fortifications was probably to accommodate military garrisons and to guard dangerous political prisoners. Last but not least, various small fortifications were erected at crossroads, often consisting of a two-storey tower built on a *proteichisma* (defensive outworks), sometimes surrounded by a wall. Clearly the purpose of these fortifications was not defence itself, but control of the main highways of the kingdom. Most of these small fortifications were renovated and partly rebuilt following the same design during Herod's reign.

City walls

At the start of the long period of Ptolemaic rule (307–198 BC), new city walls that fulfilled modern defensive needs were already being built. The period is characterized by the erection of city walls in most of the Phoenician coastal cities, as seen at Ptolemais and Dora, areas that were closer to and more receptive to Hellenistic influence. In some cities of the interior new city walls were also erected, but most of these comprised colonies or new foundations, such as Philoteria, Samaria and Marissa. Other pre-existing sites, such as

Shechem and Jerusalem, still maintained their original city walls; if new ones were built they mostly followed the existing building techniques and style.

The Ptolemaic period marked a noticeable change in the design of city walls. Improvements and innovations in warfare and siege techniques created new challenges for defensive systems. While most city walls in the land of Israel prior to the Hellenistic period were built of sun-dried mud bricks set on stone foundations, the introduction of improved battering rams, long-range missiles and artillery compelled military engineers to take careful defensive measures. City walls needed to be built from more durable and shock-resistant material, and new ways needed to be found to permit the mounting of defence artillery on the upper levels of the towers and city walls. Most of the cities now built their walls of stone; brick walls were used only where clay was abundant, and where the transportation of stone was more expensive than the city could afford. The Phoenician stone-dressing tradition dating back to the Iron Age remained unchanged. Ashlar dressing was commonly used. Thus the Macedonian builders of Samaria could still use the dressed stone of the Israelite Acropolis of Shomeron built by Achab in the eighth century BC. However, a new type of stone dressing developed in the mid second century BC. Stones were cut with façades showing bosses and polished margins on all sides, and not only on one vertical and one horizontal side as during the Iron Age and at the beginning of this period. The blocks were normally laid and set in walls according to the 'headers and stretchers' tradition, as in the walls of Hasmonaean fortifications. Generally, on flat terrain city walls followed the city's trace. On hilly sites, as in Hasmonaean Jerusalem, there is a curious incongruity between the town plan and the city walls: while the city's shape maintained a rigid orthogonal system, the city walls seemed to take topographical features into consideration. The reason for this distinction lies in the strategies for defending cities.

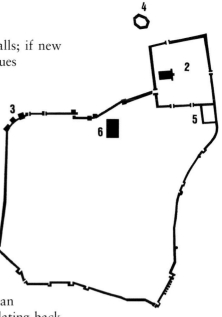

A plan of Hasmonaean Jerusalem, c. 63 BC. 1 – First Wall, 2 – Temple Mount, 3 – Western Citadel, 4 – Baris fortress, 5 – possible location of the Akra, 6 – Hasmonaean Palace. (Courtesy of Dalit Weinblatt–Krausz)

Towers and gateways

The most outstanding feature introduced into the defensive systems of the Hellenistic period was the tower. In response to new military developments, towers were improved and became military devices with independent functions. They could be built in a round form disconnected from the city walls, or as part of the wall in a round or square shape. From the Hellenistic period onwards, towers were not only used to resist attacks but also to provide artillery support for the settlement, with missile-firing devices mounted on their upper floors. The use of artillery also dramatically changed the shape of their upper part: towers were no longer crenellated, but roofed over. Two types of tower were in use in southern Coele-Syria during the Hellenistic period: round and square. Square towers were to be found in Hasmonaean Jerusalem, together with bastions; the distance between the towers does not seem to exceed 50m.

A new type of city gate appeared in the 3rd century BC. The 'courtyard city gate' was set back from the line of the wall, so that an enemy approaching the gate had to pass between two towers and across a small courtyard before reaching the gate. This type of gate had a direct axial passage, and involved indenting the line of the city walls to form a courtyard in front of the gate.

This Hasmonaean tower formed part of the northern stretch of the First Wall in Jerusalem, and stood near a gate. Note the use of unhewn stones. (Author's photograph)

Often this would be enclosed by a second gate at the outer end. The main defensive effort, however, was still put into the two strong towers flanking the entrance of the outer gate. Hellenistic city gates are not well known in southern Coele-Syria. A second type of gate was developed in the latter half of the 2nd century BC. This type consisted of an entrance between two overlapping stretches of wall, as seen in Jerusalem.

The walls of Jerusalem
The First Wall of Jerusalem was the greatest building project during the Hasmonaean period, built in the middle of the 2nd century BC by Jonathan and completed by Simon. Josephus describes the First Wall in detail (Josephus, *War* V, 142–145 and 159): he writes that this wall included no fewer than 60 towers, although some of them were probably bastions. The wall began in the area of today's Citadel, which at the time consisted of three towers (the northernmost two were actually bastions while only the southernmost was a tower). The course of the wall continued southwards, running within Mount Zion, where what Josephus calls the Essene Gate stood. The wall then turned eastwards until it reached the southernmost slopes of the City of David, which were included in the city walls, where the Siloam Pool dam–wall was located. This wide dam was reinforced by a series of pillars, and the city wall passed over the top of it. From there the wall continued northwards following the upper slopes of the eastern part of the City of David. Two towers were located here, laid down in a manner that prevented the enemy from reaching the structure's foundations. The north-eastern part of the First Wall was dominated by the Temple Mount *temenos* (sacred area), which at this time comprised a square enclosure of 280 square metres. On the north-western corner of the Temple Mount enclosure stood the Baris fortress, probably built at the end of the Persian period. The northern part of the Hasmonaean city wall ran westwards from the western part of the Temple Mount to the Citadel. A tower and a gate are all that remain today of the northern part of the First Wall. The tower was shaped like the Greek letter π, and the walls consisted of medium-sized ashlar. A gap between the line of the wall (4.6m thick) and that of a parallel fragment suggests that a city gate, possibly the Gennath Gate,

The south-eastern part of Jerusalem was dominated by the so-called City of David, shown here in reconstruction. This was in fact the early Bronze Age Jebusite city. In the Herodian period it seems that this part of the city was dominated by the Palace of the Queen of Adiabene as well as the Siloam Pool, the main water reserves in the city until the Hasmonaeans built their siphon. (The Jerusalem Model, courtesy of the Holyland Hotel)

may have been located here. The Hasmonaeans also erected a fortified palace not far from the northern segment of the First Wall (Josephus, *Antiquities* XX, 189–192, *War* II, 344).

Forts and watchtowers

Together with city walls, the main characteristics of the fortifications of the Hellenistic period built in southern Coele-Syria comprise forts and watchtowers. Most of the forts were built on sites in the interior far from the coast that had flourished in earlier periods such as the Iron Age or during Persian rule. The citadel of Beth Zur built in the late 4th century BC is probably the best example. It continued the established traditions employed in the selection of sites for fortresses, being situated on a well-protected hillock and at an important road junction, naturally leading it to develop into a town too. This fortress still featured mud-brick walls, but the Maccabaean uprising brought great changes to this and other sites, forcing the Seleucid overlords to build a series of fortifications in their attempts to contain the Maccabaean armies. In 162 BC the Seleucid general Bacchides built various strongholds at Jericho, Emmaus, Beth Horon, Bethel, Thamnatha, Pharathon and Tephon, the fortified village of Beth Zur, and the citadel of Gazara in Judaea. In these new regional fortifications, military concerns were addressed to a greater degree than before, incorporating better defensive systems against artillery, battering rams and missiles.

The best-known fortification was the Akra in Jerusalem, which was in fact begun by Antiochus III (See *First Maccabees* 9, 50–2, and Josephus, *Antiquities* XIII, 15–17). Its main characteristic was that from its towers it was possible to control the Temple Mount. In 141 BC the Akra was taken by Simon and razed to the ground. The hilltop on which the fortress was built was removed, and thus today the exact location of the Akra is unknown. Some scholars (Smith, Schürer and Simons) place the Akra in the Lower City, on the south-eastern hill of Jerusalem, following Josephus. Others scholars (Robinson, Warren, Vincent and Avi Yona) prefer to locate it in the Upper City, overlooking the Temple area and the Tyropoeon Valley. However, this view is untenable if we consider that the western hill was only included in the city in the Hasmonaean period. Zafrir's location of the Akra is probably the correct one. According to him, the Akra stood south-east of the original Temple Mount, just north of the 'seam' of the Eastern Wall of the Temple Mount; the 'seam', 32m north of the south-east corner of the Herodian podium, comprises the join between a huge masonry construction dating to Herod's time and the corner of an earlier Hellenistic structure. Meir ben Dov locates the Akra *c*. 40m south of the modern southern wall of the Temple Mount. A plastered pool found there was considered a part of the courtyard of the fortress. Ben Dov thus suggests two possibilities for reconstruction. The first consists of a small, square building with the pool in the middle of the courtyard, and four towers on the corners. The second possibility consists of a greater building extending northwards with two courtyards and six towers. The towers would have to be no less than 20m high to be capable of controlling the Temple Mount precinct.

From the outset, the Hasmonaeans made good use of fortifications. Thus, in 165 BC, after the conquest of Jerusalem, Judah Maccabaeus had walls with towers erected around Mount Zion, fortified the Temple Mount, and outside Jerusalem refortified the citadel of Beth Zur (*First Maccabees* 4, 60; and Josephus, *Antiquities* XII, 326). After Judah's death, Jonathan, his brother and heir, continued the struggle, and one of his first acts was to fortify Beth Bazi (*First Maccabees* 9, 62 and Josephus, *Antiquities* XIII, 26). In the 1st century BC the Hasmonaeans introduced a new type of fortress. Convenience gave way to inaccessible and impregnable locations, a factor sometimes overemphasized as at Alexandrium, Hyrcania and Machaerous. The Hasmonaeans also erected a fortified palace in Jerusalem (Josephus, *Antiquities* XX, 189–192, *War* II, 344). All these fortresses featured stone walls, and, lacking springs, sophisticated cisterns. Located far from strategic roads, or in places that did not afford a commanding view of the area, these fortifications were unable to prevent impending threats, as in 63 BC when Pompey invaded the Hasmonaean kingdom. In the events that followed it seems that the various forts did not play significant roles. Josephus is a good source for the late period (*Antiquities*

XIII, 422); he gives us a list of 22 fortifications that featured prominently in the civil war between Hyrcanus II and the pretender Aristobulus II, the latter dominating most of the fortifications of the kingdom. It seems that the Hasmonaean state in its last years controlled around 30 fortifications, mainly in Judaea. Although these did not play an important part in the confrontation between Pompey and Aristobulus II in 63 BC, the successive failed *coup d'état* of his two sons, Alexander and Antigonus, against Gabinius were based around control of the fortifications.

Herodian fortifications
Evolution and function
In 37 BC, after the conquest of Jerusalem, Herod could truly consider himself 'master in his own home', and it was at this point that he probably began to take care of the standing system of defence of the kingdom. The example of Jerusalem is striking. In 63 BC Pompey conquered the city after an active siege, and its fortifications were dismantled. Later, Hyrcanus II rebuilt these fortifications, at least in part, and in 40 BC the last Hasmonaean ruler, his nephew Mattathias Antigonus, entrenched himself in the city and awaited the onslaught of Herod and his Roman allies. The three years of war against Antigonus included various sieges and the capture of cities and fortresses, and thus many fortifications stood in ruin or suffering from neglect. In the period going from 37 to 32 BC Herod faced two main external threats: a possible Parthian invasion (more likely since the defeat of Antony), and Cleopatra, his powerful southern neighbour. The Nabataeans also in wait, ready to gain from any internal discord in Herod's kingdom. The internal situation was no better, as Herod's kingdom was no doubt infested with ex-soldiers turned brigands that threatened the local populations and their economies. In this period Herod probably repaired most of the Hasmonaean fortifications, without adding any new ones.

A plan of Herodian Jerusalem, c. AD 44. 1 – First Wall, 2 – Second Wall, 3 – Third Wall, 4 – Temple Mount, 5 – Antonia fortress, 6 – Herodian Citadel (comprising the Phasael, Hyppicus and Mariamne towers). (Courtesy of Dalit Weinblatt–Krausz)

In 32 BC the situation dramatically changed. The war between Octavian (later, Augustus) and Antony led Herod to become an ally of Octavian, and in a more secure and respected position than before. His victory in the war against the Nabataeans also enlarged his territory considerably. Moreover, in the period from 32 to 10 BC Augustus added various territories to the kingdom of his faithful ally, mainly to the north. It was a period in which Herod moved to modify dramatically the defensive system of his kingdom. The situation beyond his borders had also changed; late in Augustus's reign, Rome established a *modus vivendi* with Parthia, and following Cleopatra's death Egypt had become a province of Rome. The fierce Nabataean desert warriors, however, were still smarting from the huge losses of territory occurred in the last war, and as ruler of Gaza, Herod now also dominated the length of the King's Highway, the last tract of the long spice route from Nabataea. Last but not least, both the king's generosity, and the fact that from 25 to 10 BC the kingdom was completely transformed by a huge building enterprise, ensured that internal problems faded away, at least in Judaea.

Herod now had to answer to new strategic needs. As a result, he expanded the static defence of his kingdom with the erection of two huge urban centres, various palace-fortresses, the renovation of existing fortifications, and the

Herodian Judaea, c. 30 BC

implanting of colonies, scattered mainly in the unruly north facing Ituraean brigands, and in the south in Idumaea facing the Nabataeans.

A third period of evolution took place between 10 and 4 BC, characterized by the slow and ongoing work to complete all Herod's building projects. The difficult but successful Nabataean war of 8 BC did not bring about any modifications to the static defence of the kingdom. After Herod's death, his descendants continued to follow his policy. His son Antipas transformed the small garrison city of Sepphoris into a large centre, the first capital of his kingdom, and later founded Tiberias, the new capital and Livias. His grandson Agrippa I erected the Third Wall of Jerusalem.

A concluding remark needs to be made about the use of fortifications during the Jewish War of AD 66–73. Today historians agree that there was no coordinated effort by the Jews against the Romans. The central government lacked authority from the beginning, and was soon toppled by the Zealots, and Josephus's efforts to coordinate the defence of Galilee ended in total failure. Josephus clearly states that he wished to organize an army similar to that of the Romans, but the general indifference of the lower strata of the population, as well as the petty jealousy among the more extremist leaders, made this impossible. Only then did he attempt a static defence based around fortresses, as his forces could not stand up to field battle. Moreover, the advantages of static defence were that it obliged the Romans to besiege each city they faced, and did not require a coordinated effort on the part of the Jews. It is thus more correct to refer to various uncoordinated rebellions in different areas of Judaea. Only at the end of the war did many of the extremist leaders, such as John of Gush Halav, gather at Jerusalem and stand united against the final Roman onslaught – and only after a bloody and costly civil war. The political division of the Jewish leadership vis-à-vis the Roman army was also reflected in the care the new revolutionary Jewish government gave to the existing fortifications. In most cases the existing fortifications were slightly repaired, but no more. The rebels had no capacity to erect new fortifications, and probably there was no real need. There are one or two exceptions, though. Josephus, before the Roman siege at Jotapata, had a new wall erected on top of the existing one. In Jerusalem the Zealots may have completed Agrippa's Third Wall. Last but not least, once the Romans broke down the fortress wall at Masada, the Zealots replaced it with earth and timber. It was an ingenious but desperate solution.

This model of Jerusalem, today in the Israel Museum, depicts the city in the last years before the Great War of AD 66–70, at the end of the Second Temple period. The three walls, the Temple Mount, the Antonia fortress, the huge Herodian Palace and the Citadel are clearly recognizable. (Courtesy of Albatross)

A reconstruction of the Herodian Citadel, in the Jerusalem Model. From left to right, the Phasael, Hyppicus and Mariamne towers. (The Jerusalem Model, courtesy of the Holyland Hotel)

The lower part of the Hyppicus tower was later incorporated into the Ottoman Citadel. The huge Herodian ashlar stones are clearly visible. (Author's photograph)

City walls

The walls of Herod's cities were not dissimilar to earlier Hellenistic city fortifications, which continued the traditional Phoenician technique of employing rectangular ashlar stones, with margins on all sides, set in headers and stretchers. In such details, the Herodian city walls continue the characteristics of earlier fortifications; indeed, in both Jerusalem and Caesarea Maritima it is impossible to distinguish between the Hellenistic phase and the Herodian–Early Roman one.

Herod inherited Jerusalem as capital of the kingdom from the Hasmonaeans. The city's growth can be clearly seen by the development of its defences, with new walls added as it grew in importance and population. Thus at the end of the Hasmonaean period the First Wall protected an area of 165 acres, and the city contained around 30,000–35,000 inhabitants. At the time of Herod's death the city extended over a surface of 230 acres and numbered 40,000 inhabitants. Fifty years later, at the time of Agrippa I, Jerusalem's surface area had doubled, extending over 450 acres, and with a population peaking at around 80,000 inhabitants. Herodian Jerusalem included the First Wall and the Second Wall, the latter probably built by Herod, although it is possible that one of the last Hasmonaeans rulers did so.

The First Wall under Herod's rule was very similar to the original Hasmonaean construction. However, on the site of today's Citadel, three Hasmonaean towers were demolished to make way for three multi-storeyed towers, the Phasael, Mariamne and Hyppicus. Moreover, Herod rebuilt the Temple Mount. Its shape was a huge trapezoid, with the retaining walls measuring 315m on the north side, 280m on the south side, 485m on the west side and 460m on the east side. On the north-western corner of the Temple Mount, on the site of the Baris, Herod erected the Antonia fortress.

Josephus describes the Second Wall in detail. The Second Wall began at the Gennath Gate (situated in the First Wall) and ended at the Antonia fortress, at the north-western corner of the Temple Mount. Fourteen towers stood along the Second Wall (*War* V, 146, 159). It is commonly agreed that the Second Wall ran alongside a line north of the First Wall, in the area today occupied by the Christian and Muslim quarters in the northern part of the Old City. However, the surface of the area reveals no prominent topographical features that might indicate its course. Some reconstruct it along a line running north from the First Wall to the Damascus Gate, where it turned south-east and continued on towards the Antonia; others are less ambitious (having the Third Wall coincide with the present northern wall of the Old City, along the Damascus Gate) and trace the line of the Second Wall from a point just north of the Gennath Gate, turning eastwards to the Antonia fortress, and leading to a certain point south of the Damascus Gate.

The Third Wall was built by Agrippa I between AD 41 and 44. It is possible that it was left uncompleted, and its building was terminated by the Jews in AD 66. It is described by Josephus (*War* V, 147, 156–59). The wall was erected to encompass the northern part of the city that developed in the early 1st century AD. This area of the city actually stood on a plateau, which was

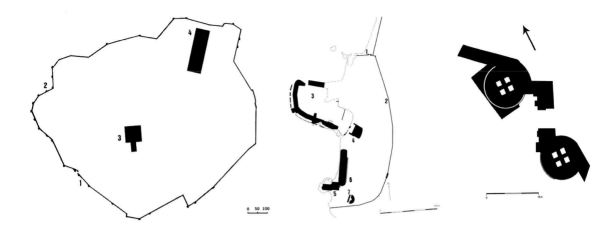

difficult to defend. The Third Wall ran northwards from the Hyppicus tower to the Psephinus tower in the west of the city, passed opposite the tomb of Queen Helene and the Royal Cave, bypassed Fuller's Monument, touched the First Wall of the Temple Mount and descended to the Kidron Valley. Remains of the Third Wall have been excavated to the east and west of the American consulate in the east of the city. The Psephinus tower (Josephus, *War* V, 160) was the most impressive tower in the Third Wall, and probably in all the city walls. It was probably very similar to the Tour Magne built as part of the fortifications of the city wall of Nemausus (Nîmes), clearly indicating a Roman origin.

New cities

The other two major urban structures of the kingdom were both founded by Herod: Sebaste, founded in 25 BC on the site of Hellenistic Samaria begun 40 years earlier by Pompey, and Caesarea Maritima, founded in 23 BC on the site of the Hellenistic city of Straton's Tower. Both cities had a mixed population of Jews and Greeks, and like Jerusalem enjoyed the status of royal cities from the beginning.

Sebaste had a clearly Gentile character, but this could not conceal the fact that the city comprised a huge garrison, being a settlement of veterans. The defences of the city protected the royal residence, but these were also a warning to the surrounding Samaritans. The irregular city area was larger than that of the Hellenistic city, at *c.* 160 acres. The encircling city wall measured around 4km, and was constructed beyond the old lines; it was built with courses of headers and stretchers on the external sides, and filled with a core of rubble. If the towers were built at roughly 50m apart from each other, then the city wall would have had at least 80 towers. As in Jerusalem,

TOP LEFT
A plan of Herodian Sebaste, *c.* 20 BC. 1 – Western Gate, 2 – city wall, 3 – Temple of Augustus, 4 – stadium.

TOP MIDDLE
A plan of Caesarea Maritima, *c.* 10 BC. 1 – Northern Gate, 2 – Herodian city wall, 3 – Sebastos, the harbour, 4 – Temple of Roma and Augustus, 5 – Herod's Promontory Palace, 6 – hippodrome, 7 – theatre.

TOP RIGHT
A plan of the Western Gate of Sebaste, *c.* AD 44. This gate was flanked by two round towers.

BOTTOM LEFT
A plan of the Northern Gate of Caesarea Maritima, *c.* 10 BC. This gate was similar to the Western Gate of Sebaste, being flanked by two round towers.

BOTTOM RIGHT
A plan of the Southern Gate of Tiberias, probably erected by the tetrarch Herod Antipas. (All plans courtesy of Dalit Weinblatt–Krausz)

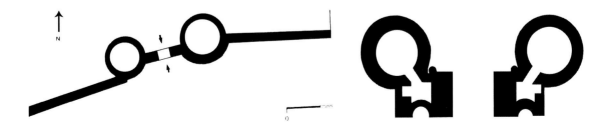

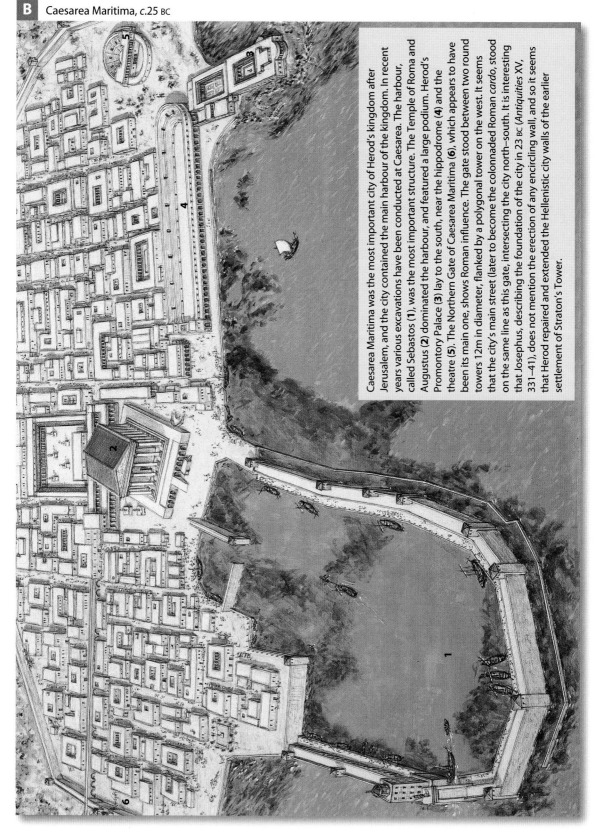

Caesarea Maritima was the most important city of Herod's kingdom after Jerusalem, and the city contained the main harbour of the kingdom. In recent years various excavations have been conducted at Caesarea. The harbour, called Sebastos (**1**), was the most important structure. The Temple of Roma and Augustus (**2**) dominated the harbour, and featured a large podium. Herod's Promontory Palace (**3**) lay to the south, near the hippodrome (**4**) and the theatre (**5**). The Northern Gate of Caesarea Maritima (**6**), which appears to have been its main one, shows Roman influence. The gate stood between two round towers 12m in diameter, flanked by a polygonal tower on the west. It seems that the city's main street (later to become the colonnaded Roman *cardo*, stood on the same line as this gate, intersecting the city north–south. It is interesting that Josephus, describing the foundation of the city in 23 BC (*Antiquities* XV, 331–41), does not mention the erection of any encircling wall, and so it seems that Herod repaired and extended the Hellenistic city walls of the earlier settlement of Straton's Tower.

Herod erected a fortified castle on the acropolis, which included a palace complex with storerooms and a temple dedicated to Augustus.

Caesarea Maritima, founded as the main harbour of the kingdom, played a more and more important role from Herod's reign onwards. After the deposition of Archelaus, the Roman governor took this city as his chief residence, and Agrippa I made this city the second of his kingdom. After the destruction of Jerusalem, Caesarea Maritima became the undisputed home of the Roman governor. It is interesting that Josephus, describing the foundation of the city in 23 BC (*Antiquities* XV, 331–41), does not mention the erection of any encircling wall. In fact it seems that Herod repaired and extended the Hellenistic city walls of the earlier settlement of Straton's Tower. In the southern part of the city it seems that the theatre, the hippodrome, the huge Temple of Roma and Augustus and the royal palace stood inside the city fortifications. The most important structure at Caesarea Maritima was the fortified harbour of Sebastos.

The Herodian dynastic rulers continued the policy of urbanization in their respective parts of Herod's kingdom. Antipas made Sepphoris, a small walled settlement, the capital of his kingdom, and later built the city of Tiberias, founded during the rule of Tiberius (Josephus, *Antiquities* XVIII 36–38). Josephus does not mention the erection of any city wall, but archaeological excavations have confirmed its existence. The wall surrounded the city on

LEFT
A plan of the Damascus Gate in Jerusalem. This was in fact the gate of the northern part of the city wall of Aelia Capitolina, erected on the ruins of Herodian Jerusalem. However, the previous Herodian gate, destroyed in the events of AD 70, followed a similar plan.

BOTTOM LEFT
The Damascus Gate, Jerusalem. The gate erected in the Ottoman period was very similar to the much earlier Roman example. (Author's photograph)

BOTTOM RIGHT
Most Roman gates contained three vaulted openings, one for the main road, and two more for each walkway. The exit shown here stood on the eastern side of the main opening of the Roman gate excavated underneath the Damascus Gate. The Roman gate, erected in the time of Hadrian, followed a similar plan to the original Herodian gate. (Author's photograph)

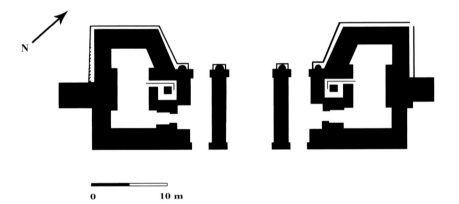

N

0   10 m

A reconstruction of the Damascus Gate as it appeared in the Herodian period. This gate was probably the main one of the Second Wall. (The Jerusalem Model, courtesy of the Holyland Hotel)

three sides, the fourth (eastern) side being the Galilee seashore. Both the northern side (*c.* 500m) and the southern side (*c.* 300 m) were comparatively short, while the western side, parallel to the Sea of Galilee, was *c.* 1, 750km long. Spacing the towers at 50m intervals, the northern part of the city wall would have had 10 towers, the western 35, and the southern six.

Gateways

It seems that, in some particulars, Herodian city walls show certain Roman influences, mainly in the towers and in the city gate. The Roman gate of the Augustan period, taken by Herod as a model, generally had three entrances covered by arches, with the middle one larger than those to the sides. Two flanking towers protected the gate. These towers could be circular, octagonal or square shaped. As per Hellenistic city gates, this type of gate had a direct axial passage. One important difference from the former was that the Roman gate had a courtyard jutting inward, not outward. The contemporary gates of Augusta Praetoria, Augusta Taurinorum and Verona seem to have influenced Herodian gates, which were thus characterized by a central arched gate flanked by two square (Jerusalem) or round (Caesarea Maritima, Tiberias) side towers.

It is possible that the gate excavated under the present-day Damascus Gate in Jerusalem, probably the main gate of the Second Wall, was in origin a three-arched one flanked by two square towers. The gate underlying the Damascus Gate was erected by the Romans who built the colony of Aelia Capitolina. However, its foundations consisted of three openings between two projecting towers. The gate was built of Herodian ashlar with drafted margins in secondary use. In the foundations of the western tower, archaeologists exposed remains of an earlier wall, built of large ashlar blocks; the section consisted of a corner at an obtuse angle. Hamilton dated the wall to the Herodian period, thus making it likely that the Herodian city gate was built prior to the Roman gate of Aelia Capitolina.

The Western Gate of Sebaste sported two round towers, each 14m in diameter, which flanked the entrance. The two towers protruded from the wall, as did the 11m-diameter round tower located 53m north of the northern tower of the gate. Another gate that shows Roman influence is the Northern Gate of Caesarea Maritima. It stood between two 12m-diameter round towers, flanked by a polygonal tower to the west. It seems that on the same line of this gate stood the city's main street, later to become the colonnaded Roman *cardo*, that bisected the city north–south.

The Southern Gate of Tiberias was built by Antipas, Herod's son, using well-dressed basalt stone. Two 7m-diameter round towers, projecting to the south, flanked the gate. Two niches flanked the entrance inside the gate building. Two pedestals were set between the round towers and the door jambs in front of the gate; the pedestals supported columns and were decorated with rhombuses in relief. The *cardo* led from the exit of the gate.

Fortified palaces
Herod erected various fortified palaces after 32 BC. These fortifications can be divided into two types. The first type consists of citadels or fortified palaces located in cities, as exemplified by the Citadel's towers and the Antonia in Jerusalem, and the acropolis of Sebaste. The purpose of these citadels was to defend the king during the siege of the city by an exterior enemy, or to protect the king against possible internal rebellions by his subjects. It is interesting to note that in the classical world social unrest always began in the cities, not in the countryside. The second type of

A reconstruction of the Herodian Temple Mount and the Antonia fortress. On the left is the Third Wall leading from the Temple Mount, and on the right is the Antonia fortress. (The Jerusalem Model, courtesy of the Holyland Hotel)

C NEXT PAGE: THE TEMPLE MOUNT AND ANTONIA FORTRESS, c. AD 44

The Temple Mount, which Herod had rebuilt, was shaped like a huge trapezoid, with the retaining walls measuring 315m on the north side (**1a**), 280m on the south side (**1b**), 485m on the west side (**1c**), and 460m on the east (**1d**). On the north-western corner of the site, on the former site of the Baris (destroyed many years before this date), Herod erected the Antonia fortress (**2**), one of the most important in his kingdom, at some point after 31 BC. Josephus describes it in detail (*Antiquities* XVIII, 91–95, and *War* V,

238–46). Its four square towers, one of which was taller than the others, were situated at its corners and dominated the Temple. The interior of the fortress was designed and furnished as a palace. According to Netzer, the Antonia fortress was the prototype for the palace-fortress of Herodium, which differed only in its circular plan. Its purpose was to withstand a siege from a hostile army, as opposed to the threat posed by rebellious subjects. The fortress was destroyed by the Romans in AD 70.

construction consists of fortified palaces or castles that were scattered all around the kingdom. Some of them were situated at the sites of important administrative centres, like Herodium. Other fortifications, such as Masada, were situated in accessible areas, far from any urban centres.

The common task of these fortifications was to protect the person of the king, his family and his retinue. These fortifications could serve the king in times of war, when protected by strong ramparts, he could wait to be relieved by his own army or that of the Romans. However, these fortifications also served the king in times of peace. Often the king had to be away from the city visiting his kingdom, and his family (sometimes) and his courtiers, counsellors, officials and friends (always) would follow him on his travels. Thus, within the kingdom's borders there was a real need for heavily fortified sites that could host the king, his family, his chief officials and his court – in all its magnificence and pomp. As a consequence, the king's show of magnificence was not just restricted to the capital, and he could attend to administrative duties and take decisions whenever needed. There was also a slightly different motivation. As king, Herod was also the supreme judge in the country, and the capacity to make judgments in far-off corners of his kingdom for the benefit of the local population could only improve his popularity.

Herod chose the tetrapyrgion (a towered palace) as the main model for both types of fortifications. This type of fortification originated in the Hellenistic world (probably in Asia Minor in the 4th century BC) and comprises a fortress with towers on the outside, built on the highest hill in the area. The inside was furnished with luxurious elements of domestic architecture. The earliest example of a tetrapyrgion is probably the Palace of

A reconstruction of the Psephinus tower, which dominated the Third Wall. (The Jerusalem Model, courtesy of the Holyland Hotel)

Mausolus at Halicarnassus. Upper Herodium and the Antonia in Jerusalem share the same features as the Hellenistic tetrapyrgion, the main difference between the two Herodian fortresses being that Herodium follows a circular plan, while the Antonia has a rectangular one. The fortified palaces in Jerusalem were built on the same sites as earlier Hasmonaean fortifications that originally had different purposes, as these buildings did not serve as royal residences. The Citadel in Jerusalem was built on three Hasmonaean towers that formed part of the First Wall. The Antonia was probably built on the site of the Baris fortress. The latter had only defensive purposes, and served as royal residence only during siege.

Multi-storey towers

Towers constitute an important part of the Herodian architectural range. The Pharos of Alexandria and the huge siege tower of Demetrius Poliorcetes provide the Hellenistic architectural models. These buildings were multi-storeyed towers with a clear functional purpose. The former was a lighthouse and the second a siege tower. These towers were adapted by Herod and transformed into palaces. The Mariamne, Phasael and Hyppicus towers in Jerusalem were multi-storeyed examples with residential functions. The Antonia and Herodium fortresses had larger, multi-storeyed towers with the same function. The main difference between the first and the last groups is their architectural setting: the towers around Herod's palace in Jerusalem are independent units, whereas the Herodium and Antonia towers are part of an architectural complex. In Herodian architecture, many multi-storeyed towers also held a functional purpose; the Drusium tower in the Caesarea Maritima harbour served as a lighthouse.

In Jerusalem, a citadel with three huge towers was built north of Herod's palace, at the north-west corner of the city wall. The towers were named Hyppicus, Phasael and Mariamne after Herod's friend, brother and wife respectively. Josephus gives a vivid description (*War* V, 156–76) of these constructions. The Hyppicus tower was square. On top of the first storey (which was solid) there was a water reservoir, with a palace across two storeys divided into several parts above this. The palace was crowned with battlements and turrets. The second tower, the Phasael, consisted of a solid square base, topped by a peristyle (open colonnade), surrounded by bulwarks. On the top of the peristyle building stood another smaller tower, divided into various rooms and a bathhouse. This upper tower was topped with battlements. The third tower, the Mariamne, was similar to the other two in that it had a solid base and was topped by a second decorated storey. Only the base of one of the towers has survived. It is 21m in length, 17m in width, and has a solid foundation. This was a multi-storeyed tower, and has been identified by scholars as being either the Hyppicus or Phasael.

Josephus also provides us with a detailed description of the Antonia fortress (*Antiquities* XVIII, 91–95 and *War* V, 238–46). This fortress was rebuilt by Herod before 31 BC and is named after Antony. It was situated close to the north-west corner of the Temple Mount, and dominated the Temple. Four square towers, one of which was taller than the others, were situated at the corners. The interior of the fortress was designed and furnished as a palace, as described by Josephus. According to Netzer, the Antonia fortress was the prototype for the palace-fortress of Herodium, which differs only in its circular plan. Clearly, the purpose of the Antonia was to withstand a siege from a hostile army, and not rebellious subjects.

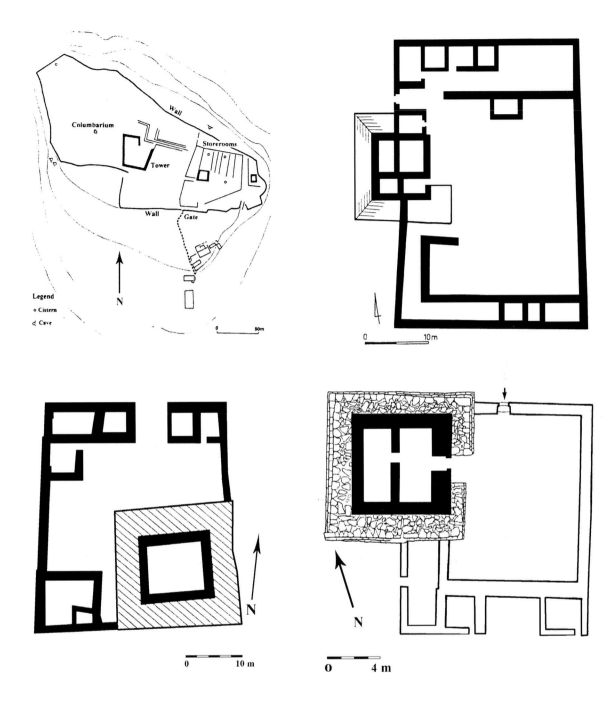

Forts, fortlets and other towers

Herod restored most of the existing forts in the parts of the kingdom where the Hasmonaeans once ruled, and probably built new fortifications, or restored old Seleucid ones, in the newly acquired northern parts of the kingdom. These fortifications served a dual purpose: to protect the surrounding area from local or regional enemies, and to serve as part of the general defence of the kingdom against a foreign invader.

Three types of fortifications can be clearly discerned, the first being forts. These buildings hosted the residence of a *stategos*, or military governor, and sometimes, in dangerous and untamed regions, were also the centre of civil administration. These fortifications were structurally similar to the fortified

Plans of Hasmonaean and Herodian smaller fortifications: clockwise from top left – Kirbet Firdusi, Rujm el-Hamiri, Ofarim and Arad. All these forts are characterized by the presence of a tower strengthened by a proteichisma. (Courtesy of Dalit Weinblatt–Krausz)

royal palaces, albeit slightly smaller. The main purpose of these types of fortifications was administrative, but in times of war could also tie down an enemy army in siege operations. These fortresses were situated throughout Herod's kingdom, and examples can be seen at Hyrcania in Judaea and Alexandrium in Samaria. However, the best example is the tetrapyrgion at Horvat 'Eleq.

The second type comprises fortlets. These buildings generally measured 22 × 22m, and were ubiquitous in Herod's kingdom. They could host a small garrison, and could thus be employed in various tasks. These fortifications were built along the borders of Herod's kingdom so that their garrisons could check local raids by foreign forces. Another task was control of the major crossroads of the kingdom, and protection of the local population against bandits. Last but not least, these fortresses were built along the coastal line, probably to control undefended spots that were vulnerable from the sea. In this task these forts served both as the primary defence against hostile sea landings and as the main point of communication with major forces of the standing army located near the spot where the fort was located.

The third type comprises towers. Towers were the smallest fortifications in the Herodian kingdom, and few have been excavated. Those that have been were primarily tasked with observation of the main roads in the kingdom. Their main characteristic was the *proteichisma*. This comprised a stone slope built around the tower, which was used to ward off enemy tunnelling and to keep battering rams away from the tower. These buildings generally measured 10 × 10m, and had two storeys. Examples of these fortresses have been excavated at Rujm el-Hamiri, Rujm el-Deir and Khirbeth el-Qasr in the Hebron Hills. These fortifications can be classed according to their region; in Judaea, Idumaea and Galilaea the population mostly consisted of non-troublesome Jews and Idumeans, whereas in Samaria, Transjordan, the coastal plain and the Decapolis the majority of the population consisted of potentially rebellious Gentiles.

A TOUR OF THE SITES

At the time of writing, not all the Hasmonaean and Herodian fortifications are accessible to the public. This chapter provides a tour of some of the most important fortifications. The best example of a Hasmonaean fortification is provided by Alexandrium, although the Herodian additions changed the plan of the fort slightly, while the best Herodian fortifications are Herodium, Masada, Machaerous and Horvat 'Eleq.

Alexandrium
Josephus (*Antiquities* XIII, 417) states that Alexandrium (Sartaba) was built by the Hasmonaeans. The fort, which commanded the route along the Jordan

D HERODIUM, c. 4 BC

1. Plan of the site, showing the artificial mound on which the upper palace-fortress was built (**a**), the location of the lower palace complex containing the administrative buildings (**b**), and the route of the stairway to the upper complex, which was buried below ground in its upper section (**c**).

2. Plan view of the palace-fortress of Upper Herodium, indicating the East Tower (**d**), peristyle courtyard (**e**), West Tower (**f**), South Tower (**g**), North Tower (**h**), and main hall (**i**).

3. Cutaway view of the partially buried upper palace-fortress, showing the concentric walls, with the East Tower clearly dominant.

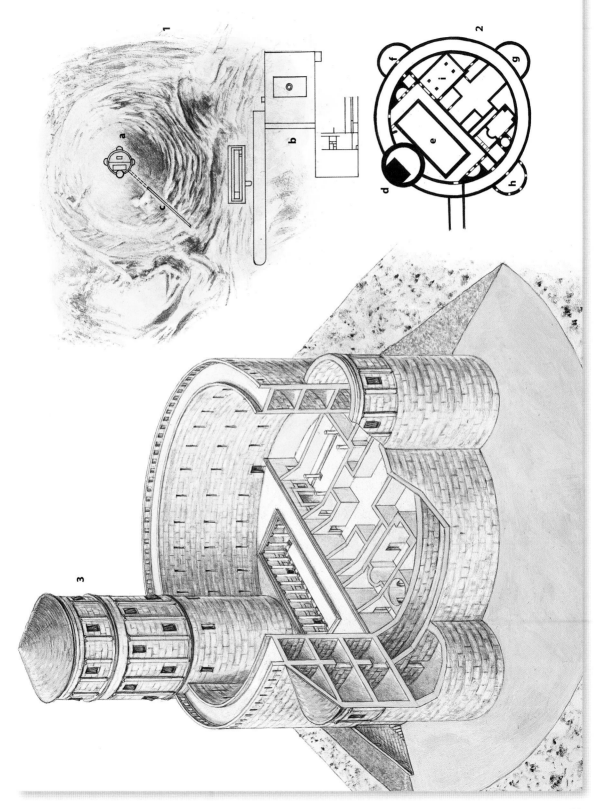

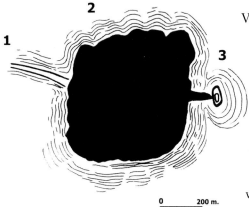

A plan of Hasmonaean and Herodian Alexandrium.
1 – aqueduct, 2 – plateau, 3 – fortress. (Courtesy of Dalit Weinblatt–Krausz)

0   200 m.

Valley, was built in the toparchy of Acraba. It was the first major Hasmonaean fortress to be restored by Herod, an undertaking given to his brother Pheroras in 38 BC (*Antiquities* XIV, 419, *War* I, 308). An ascending path leads from the main road in the valley to a western saddle in a hill. From there a zigzag path supported by retaining walls leads to the fort on the summit. The fortress extended beyond the summit (30–40m) in width and continued down the eastern slopes of the hill. The fortress contains a hall with a peristyle courtyard dating from the Hasmonaean period. A later Herodian vaulted peristyle was built on top of this.

The water supply was well organized, with several systems bringing water to the fortress. The first consisted of an aqueduct, which collected water from the Ras Quneitra plateau. A 187m-long canal built atop a ramp, and a 192m-long inverted siphon (postdating the canal) took the water from the plateau and brought it to the cisterns. The second consisted of the Ras Quneitra aqueduct. The water was collected in a series of open pools or reservoirs, comprising four cisterns on two levels on the northern slope, four cisterns on the eastern slope, and a further six cisterns on three levels on the southern slope. The total capacity was 4,800 cubic metres. During the Herodian period Alexandrium was used as a state prison for members of the royal family. Herod detained his wife Mariamne and his mother Alexandra there in 30 BC (Josephus, *Antiquities* XV, 185–86), and later on he had his sons Alexander and Aristobulus buried there following their executions at Sebastia (*Antiquities* XVI, 394). Herod showed the fortification to Marcus Agrippa during his tour of the kingdom in 15 BC (*Antiquities* XVI, 13).

Herodium

Herodium was built on the site where Herod defeated Mattathias Antigonus's force that had been sent to capture him while fleeing to Rome. It was also not far from the spot where his brother Phasael committed suicide in 40 BC (Josephus, *Antiquities* XIV, 365–69 and *War* I, 268–73). This site meant so much to Herod that he decided to be buried there, probably in a monumental tomb at the foot of the huge artificial mound on which the castle was built. Moreover, Herodium replaced Beth Zur as the administrative capital of the toparchy in the regional administration of Judaea.

The complex, which included an upper palace-fortress and a huge lower palace with various buildings, was erected in *c.* 23 BC, and Josephus has left us a vivid description (*Antiquities* XV, 324). The palace-fortress was situated on the summit of the Jebel Fureidis; its circular structure was partially buried immediately post-completion by earth and stones, giving the whole structure the shape of a tumulus (grave) and creating an artificial cone-shaped mountain. The natural hill over which the palace fortress was built rises high above the adjacent vicinity, offering a panoramic view of the landscape far around all the way to Jerusalem. It is possible that the palace-fortress of Herodium was in eye contact with its twin the Antonia, and that these fortresses could communicate with each other.

The circular palace-fortress building consisted of two massive concentric walls with an outer diameter of 63m and an inner diameter of 51m, and the three-storey high perimeter wall 3.5m wide. The circular structure of the palace-fortress had four towers, three of which were semicircular, and were situated on the northern, western and southern sides; these towers were two storeys high. The fourth, eastern tower, which was fully circular, had a diameter of 18.2m, and was used as living quarters. Both the towers and the perimeter wall had two further storeys underground, which were covered by the earth and stone glacis. The entrance, a covered gateway, lay at the eastern tower.

On each storey various siege machines could be set up. The circular shape of both the towers and the structure itself assured that there was no space uncovered by the fortress' artillery. The slope of the glacis, on the other side, assured that no siege machine could come close to the fortress. It is important to stress that this *chef d'oeuvre* of Hellenistic fortification could be justified only for use against the threat of an external regular army.

Machaerous

This fortress was situated east of the Dead Sea on the summit of the 700m-high El Mashneke hill. Strabo (*Geography* XVI, 2, 400) mentions this Hasmonaean fortification, together with the others destroyed by Pompey. The fortress was built on an area of 4,260m² on the north-eastern slope of the hill. It seems that the Hasmonaean fortress featured four towers, a central court and a ritual bathhouse. Only two towers were measured; No. 2 was 18 × 11m, and No. 3 was 18 × 14m. All the towers had internal rooms. The wall of the fortress was 1.75–2m wide. The wall and the towers were built using square blocks set irregularly. A small city lay below the fort. Its encircling wall was protected by at least two towers, tower No. 5 on the north, which measured 8 × 10m, and tower No. 6, which measured 10 × 14m. The wall of the city was 2–2.5m wide.

Herod partly rebuilt the fort, and Josephus has left us a description (*War* VII, 171–77). The Herodian fort was probably of the tetrapyrgion type, like the Antonia and Herodium, and similarly was attached to a walled city – but, it appears, there was no royal palace present. Herod probably enlarged the south-eastern side of the fortress, and storerooms were built on the eastern side of the court. Inside the fort, various elements have been excavated, including a paved peristyle court in the upper centre of the site, another paved court in the lower part, and a Roman-style bathhouse to the west of this court.

Masada

Masada is the largest and the best-known of the desert fortresses. It lies on a rock cliff about 25km south of 'En-Gedi. Josephus's description is well known (*War* VII, 8). Masada could only be approached in two places: on the east via the so-called Snake Path, and on the west where the ascent was easier. Masada already served as a fortress in the Hasmonaean period, probably having soldiers camped on the top of the cliff, living in tents. The enforced stay there by Herod's family, besieged by the Parthians from 40 to 37 BC, made this spot a future royal residence. Moreover, the fortification of Masada could also contribute to control of the Royal Highway.

Three building stages can be discerned at Masada. During the early stage, dated sometime after 37 BC, the water system as well as the core of the Western Palace, and buildings 11, 12, 13 were erected. During the second phase, dated to around 25 BC, the Northern Hanging Palace as well as the adjoining

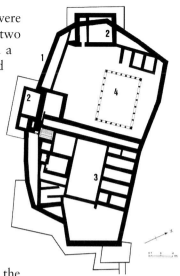

bathhouse, the new wings of the Western Palace and the storage houses were erected. During the third stage, dated around 20 BC, the casemate walls around the fortress were erected and the Western Palace took its final form.

The fortress wall had four gates, 30 towers, 70 rooms and four gates. The casemate wall encloses the plateau on all sides, except at its northern tip. Its circumference measures 1,400m, or 1,300m in a straight line. The wall is built of dolomite stone, quarried from the cliff itself and only lightly dressed. The stones were laid on the inner and outer faces with the space between them filled with smaller stones. Both sides of the wall were covered with white

A storeroom at Masada. The floors and ceilings of the storerooms were plastered with clay. (Author's photograph, with permission of the Israel Nature and Parks Authority)

plaster. The outer wall is 1.4m thick, and the inner wall 1m. The width of the casemate is about 4m. Altogether there are 70 rooms. The 6m-wide towers were built at irregular intervals, according to the terrain and for tactical reasons. The shortest distance between them is 35m, the longest 90m. Some of the towers had stairs leading to the top. Each tower had an entrance, usually near the northern partition wall. Four gates from the time of Herod were all built according to the same general plan: a square room with two entrances, one in the outer wall, and one in the inner wall, and benches along the walls. The Snake Path Gate was situated in the north-eastern sector, the Western Gate in the middle of the western wall, the Cistern Gate (Southern Gate) in the south-eastern section of the wall (150m north-east of the southern edge of the cliff), and the Water Gate (Northern Gate) in the north-west corner of the wall.

A complex of public storehouses stands in the northern complex, south of the Northern Palace. This is subdivided into two blocks: the northern block, consisting of long storerooms (20 × 3.8m), and a right-angle corridor that forms a kind of double storeroom. Each room has a single entrance in the south. The floors and ceilings of the storerooms are plastered with clay. The southern block is larger and consists of 11 elongated storerooms (27 × 4m) with entrances at the northern end. The plateau area was left for cultivation to ensure supplies for the defenders if they were cut off. Thus, the palace was abundantly stocked with corn, oil, wine, pulses and dates, and a plentiful supply of food existed for years ahead. It is interesting to note that because of the very dry climate the supplies could be preserved for a long time, and did need not to be changed or restocked.

The main issue facing the defenders of Masada was of course the water supply. When Herod left his fiancee Mariamne, his future mother-in-law and 800 soldiers in Masada in 40 BC, their main problem during the ensuing Parthian siege was thirst. The water system included a drainage system (carrying the rainwater from the wadis in the west) and two groups of cisterns in the lower part of the north-western slope (outside the walls), and another group of cisterns on the summit of the rock. The drainage system carried rainwater from the Masada Valley in the south and the Ben-Yair Valley in the north. Dams were built in both valleys, and the water flowed through gently sloping open channels into the cisterns. The well-plastered aqueduct in the Masada Valley was very wide at 1.4m and supplied water to the upper rows of pools. A second aqueduct conveyed the waters of the Ben-Yair Valley into the lower row of cisterns. The cisterns were cut into the slope in two parallel rows in the lower part of the north-western slope, with eight in the upper row and four in the lower. Most of them were square-shaped. Each cistern could hold about 4,000 cubic metres, and their total capacity was about 40,000 cubic metres. A winding path led from the upper row of cisterns to the Water Gate near the Northern Palace. Water was probably brought from the outside cisterns to the fortress using mules. The path was covered, and difficult to see from far away. Channels were dug from the Water Gate and the Snake Path to the main reservoirs. Water poured into these channels flowed into the reservoirs by force of gravity. A number of large reservoirs were also cut into the plateau of Masada, on the north, south and east sides.

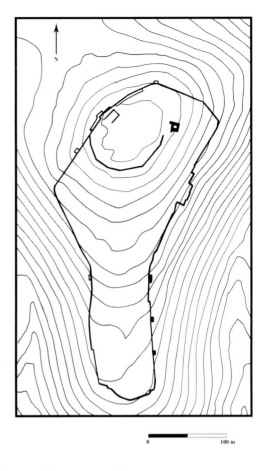

A plan of Jotapata, which clearly shows the topography of the city.

Horvat 'Eleq

The huge complex of Horvat 'Eleq is situated in the southern part of the Carmel ridge not far from the coast and some 7.5km from Caesarea Maritima. The fortress dominated Caesarea Maritima's water supply as well as the roads leading from the city to the interior of the kingdom. The complex included various elements, including a large fortified building erected at the top of a hill, and water-related and agricultural installations. Among the latter were a bathhouse in Roman style and a pool, an aqueduct, a columbarium and an oil press. The whole complex extends over a surface of three hectares. The fortification, which can be defined as a small tetrapyrgion, measures 62m along its north–south axis and 77.5m along its east–west axis. The fortress wall features four corner towers and two intermediate towers. The gate in the southern wall is flanked by two towers. In the north-western part of the courtyard stands a square tower, built on a square *proteichisma*. The tower was between 20 and 25m high, and had four or five storeys. The eastern part of the courtyard was occupied by the living quarters of the garrison.

Jotapata

The site is situated on an isolated hill in Lower Galilee near modern-day Moshav Yodefat. A third of the adjoining town was built on four to five large terraces on the steep eastern slope, with the remaining two-thirds on the southern plateau. Five residential areas have been excavated, and modest private dwellings with cisterns, ritual baths, and storage areas have been exposed. The remains of a luxurious mansion decorated with frescos attest to

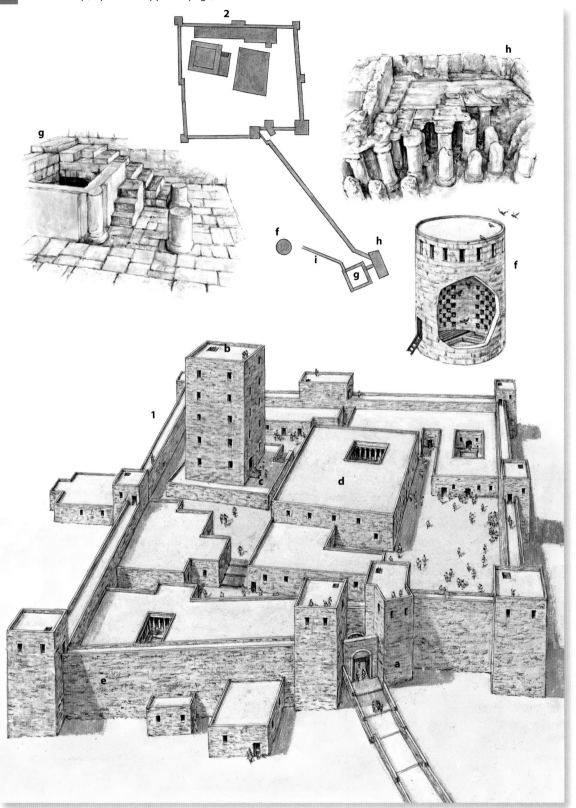

the presence of prosperous dwellers here. Josephus states that he personally fortified Jotapata, when he assumed command of the defences of Galilee.

Two phases of fortification can be differentiated on the mound's northern side, which is accessible, although it is the weakest spot in the town's natural defences. The earlier phase, which probably dates to the Hasmonaean period, consists of two parallel walls that merge into a single wall beyond the summit. A massive tower lies in the centre of the site with a smaller tower to the west. The second phase of fortification, which must be related to Josephus's efforts, can be identified in two different areas on the northern side. The first is a long, narrow wall, exposed to a length of 20m. This served as a second line of fortification behind the earlier walls. The second is a portion of a casemate wall, 4.9m wide, built above the Hasmonaean wall. Infill, comprising large boulders, near the western part of the casemate wall was probably done by the town defenders to prevent battering rams from breaking through the walls.

An aerial view of Horvat 'Eleq. The main elements of the fortress, the surrounding walls and towers, as well as the main tower and the surrounding *proteichisma* are clearly visible. (Courtesy of the late Professor Yizhar Hirschfeld, The Hebrew University of Jerusalem)

E   HORVAT 'ELEQ

1. Reconstruction of the site.
(**a**) Gate
(**b**) Tower
(**c**) *Proteichisma*
(**d**) Main building
(**e**) Outer walls

2. Plan view, showing outer buildings attached to the site.
(**f**) Columbarium (dovecote)
(**g**) Pool, with remains in inset illustration
(**h**) Bathhouse, with remains in inset illustration
(**i**) Aqueduct

Gamla

The town of Gamla is situated in the southern part of the Golan plateau, overlooking Lake Kinnereth. The city was built on a steep hill shaped like a camel's hump, from which the site's name derives (*gamla* means 'camel' in Hebrew). A wall, which extended for a length of 350m, surrounded the lower part of the town on its eastern extremity. This was in fact built on Josephus's orders and takes in a patchwork of existing buildings. Thus the wall is not entirely straight, rather it bulges, zig-zags, projects and retracts. The remaining north, south and west sides of the town were protected by the natural defences of steep slopes. Along the wall, from south to north, are two entrances, which cannot really be called gates. The first, in the southern part of the wall, is the so-called Water Gate, an opening between two square buildings, which may have been transformed into towers at the time of the rebellion. The second, the Twin Tower Gate, lies midway along the wall and consists of square twin towers; it may possibly have been built before the war as the official gate of the town. North of the wall stands a round tower, partly built using hewn stones, which dates to the Hasmonaean or to the Herodian period. This tower was probably the only original defensive element of the town. Near the northern segment of the wall, inside the city, stands the 'synagogue', or the city's main public building. This is a rectangular structure that measures 22 × 17m. The main hall is surrounded by a simple Doric colonnade, and is entered through two doors from the south-west. The corner columns are heart-shaped. West of the 'synagogue' there is an exedra (a semicircular recess) faced by a rectangular courtyard, and a ritual bath. A building immediately south of the synagogue, which is part of the city wall, shows traces of the Roman breach. Among the other features excavated at the site are an olive vat and a mansion with a ritual bath. In recent years a basilica-like building has been excavated in the upper area of the city.

BELOW
Gamla, with the outer wall and the towers clearly visible. (Courtesy of Dany Syon, Gamla excavations)

THE LIVING SITES

The Hasmonaean and the Herodian armies, like most Hellenistic and late Republican–early imperial Roman armies, were tasked with both offensive and defensive warfare. However, both the Hasmonaeans and Herod preferred to wage offensive wars against the enemy. Thus, the main constituent units of the army consisted of infantry and cavalry. These units were composed of citizens of the state who were obliged to serve in the army once the ruler called them to arms.

The organization of the Hasmonaean army was similar to that of the Seleucids, albeit on a much smaller scale. The cavalry, both light and heavy, probably made up not less than a quarter of its total strength. The infantry probably included lightly armed units of archers and slingers, semi-heavy infantry units such as the Hellenistic theurophoroi, and heavily armed infantry, organized along similar lines to the late Hellenistic phalanx. The cavalry of Herod's army were organized along similar lines to that of the Hasmonaeans. The infantry included lightly and heavily armed units, the latter moulded on the Roman model.

The main characteristic of the Hasmonaean and the Herodian armies was that the main ethnic element comprised Jews, the only state subjects who had a military obligation. Gentiles were probably exempted from this, at least in the Hasmonaean period. Because of this, the army was mainly a reserve force. The standing army in the early Hasmonaean period was probably very small, and only the last Hasmonaean ruler employed a much bigger standing army, whose core consisted of professional soldiers of local origin (Jews) who lived in military colonies, as well as foreign mercenaries (some Jews, but mostly Gentiles, Cilicians and Pisidians) who were billeted in the various fortresses of the kingdom. Herod continued this policy. Foreign mercenaries not only served in the standing army as heavy infantry and cavalry units of the Sebastenoi, or the Jewish-Babylonian cavalry unit of Zamaris, or the lightly armed Ituraean archers, but also served as the king's bodyguard. The latter was composed of Gallic, Germanic and Thracian mercenaries.

During the various offensive wars the Hasmonaean army probably developed a small corps of engineers that could plan sieges and build machines. The same no doubt applied to Herod's army, with the difference that by then this corps of engineers had become highly professional and included many Roman officers. As the siege of Jerusalem clearly shows, Herod mastered Roman siege techniques well, erecting a ring of fortifications around Jerusalem in a clear parallel to Julius Caesar's siege works around Alesia. These fortifications served two purposes: they prevented any defenders from fleeing the city, and kept any auxiliary force from coming to the aid of the besieged city.

Fortifications played an important role in the planning of defensive warfare in the Hasmonaean and Herodian periods. It is therefore essential to analyze the relationship between the various types of fortification and the type of units that defended them. It appears that the defence of the city walls was given to the citizens who dwelled in the city. The primary reason was that the local population, as everywhere in the classical world, had much to lose. Moreover, professional soldiers were expensive, and were utilized only for specific military actions, such as a sortie, or for the building of counter-fortifications – not for the everyday routine of a siege. If city walls were managed by the citizens, the citadels (for example, the Antonia and the Hyppicus, Phasael and Mariamne towers in Jerusalem) were probably defended by the king's bodyguard, as these fortifications ensured the king's security. The Temple Mount had a police guard composed of Levites, who were members of the lesser clergy and were no doubt responsible for the defence of the Temple Mount compound. It would seem logical that the main royal fortresses (such as Herodium and Masada) were also defended by a bodyguard or by mercenaries.

In peacetime the royal fortresses fulfilled another very important task, hosting the standing army of the state. At the beginning of the Hasmonaean period this was not a pressing requirement, as all the soldiers when not on reserve duty preferred to dwell in their own homes. This changed dramatically in the late Hasmonaean period, when rulers such as Alexander Jannaeus had need of small standing armies, composed of foreign mercenaries such as Cilicians and Pisidians. During Herod's reign the problem became more acute. A possible solution was to billet the soldiers in the various cities of the kingdom among the citizens, as Herod did with Roman soldiers after his conquest of Jerusalem in 37 BC. This, however, posed many problems; the citizens were unwilling to share their homes with soldiers, and it could take a long time to muster soldiers billeted in various buildings far from one another and from their officers' watchful eyes. It is interesting to note the Roman playwright Plautus's *Miles Gloriosus*, which gives us a somewhat exaggerated description of a Hellenistic mercenary of the period, via the figure of Pirgopolinix. Hasmonaean and Herodian Judaea, part of the larger Hellenistic world, would not have been very different. One possible solution was to keep the soldiers of the standing army apart from the civil population within the citadels, which were well suited to this purpose.

Smaller fortifications were probably defended by military colonists, who were well motivated for the defence of the immediate surroundings where they had settled. The fortlets controlled the roads, warded off brigands and acted as toll stations. Colonies generally consisted of agricultural settlements, often situated near the frontier or in newly conquered terrain. Hellenistic sovereigns, including the Hasmonaeans and Herod, generally gave each colonist (*katoikos*) an allotment of agricultural land (*kleros*) to maintain himself and his family in times of peace, and to provide himself with the weapons needed for his task and rank during war. The colonists lived in the countryside either in isolation or grouped in villages. The organization and exact whereabouts of the Hasmonaean colonies remain unknown. According to Josephus, Herod settled more than 12,000 military colonists. He reports that Herod settled 3,000 Idumaeans in Trachonitis (*Antiquities* XVI, 285), 600 men under Zamaris in Batanaea (*Antiquities* XVII, 24), an unnumbered quantity of horsemen (probably no more than 1,000) in Hesebon (*Antiquities* XV, 293–96) and Gabae (*Antiquities* XV, 294 and *War* III, 36), 6,000 colonists in Samaria (*Antiquities* XV, 296, and *War* I, 403), and 2,000 Idumaeans in Idumaea (*War* II, 55). To the best of our knowledge, no colony was ever founded in Judaea proper.

The colony (of 3,000 Idumaeans) founded in the north-eastern part of Trachonitis was established after a rebellion of local Ituraeans. The colony was destroyed in 10–9 BC during a later rebellion, and probably re-established. The primary purpose of the colony was to have a group of loyal soldiers on the spot, veterans who could quell any local attempt at rebellion; the Idumaeans, Herod's kinsmen, clearly represented a loyal element in his kingdom. Another possible purpose of the colony was, over the long term, to foster Idumaean interbreeding with the local population, bringing it closer to the fold of Judaism and making the area more secure by peaceful means. These settled colonists would also have provided an example of settled living to the still nomadic Idumaeans, thus addressing the source of the problem.

The Batanean colony (named Bathyra) lay in the northern territories of Herod's kingdom. All of the colonists were Babylonian Jews (another loyal group) who had settled there with their leader, Zamaris. This colony probably served the same purpose as the other colonies, keeping the local population in check, and guarding the border against nomadic incursions.

In Galilee Herod founded the famous colony of Gabae. According to Gracey the colony was founded to check possible insurrection on the part of the Jewish population. The colonists themselves may have been Jews. In Galilee a considerable part of the population was Gentile, and the question arises as to why a colony was not founded to control them. Galilee was a region in which brigands were always a serious problem. It is possible that the main purpose of the colony was to keep brigands and outlaws, Jew and Gentile alike, in check.

In Samaria Herod distributed plots of land to 6,000 men. According to Gracey the main purpose of these colonies would have been to protect Jerusalem and Judaea. However, Samaria was a separate region and one might have expected Herod to found colonies in Judaea instead. Herod probably had the unruly Samaritans in mind rather than the Jews. He selected Gentile colonists and not Jews, as settling Jews here would have certainly aggravated the existing religious tensions between Jews and Samaritans.

The purpose of the colony of horsemen founded in Hesebon was probably to keep the local population in check, protect the Jewish settlers, and contribute to the defence of the region against the Nabataeans.

Various colonies were founded in Idumaea by Herod. It is striking that the colonists (comprising some 2,000 Idumaean veterans) were of the same stock as the local population. The sole possible purpose of a colony in Idumaea would have been to keep the Nabataeans at bay, as it is unlikely that soldiers of the same stock as the local population would quell any attempted rebellion by the locals.

Several questions concerning the Herodian military colonies remain open. It is unclear whether these were infantry or cavalry colonies, but they would appear to have included both: Idumaeans were known in the classical period as light infantrymen, while other elements among the colonists were cavalrymen, as, for example, the colonists of Bathyra. From the data that we have, the model for the Herodian colonies appears to have been a Hellenistic rather than a Roman one. The Herodian colonies appear to have followed a clear Seleucid precedent of settling veterans together in villages.

It is interesting to analyze the relationship between the rebels and the local population during the Jewish War. First of all it is important to recall that the central revolutionary Jewish government did not succeed in creating a unified and coordinated Jewish army; in each area, the rebels acted independently. Thus, the local populations often had to cope with different and often mutually hostile groups of rebels, a difficulty reflected in the relationship between the populations and the rebels. For example, in many cases in Galilee various cities, such as Sepphoris, did not take part in the war, but sided with the Romans from the outset. In other cases, such as at Gamla, there was close collaboration between the local population and the rebels; however, it seems that the rebels were few in number, and were local figures that took care of the population. The result was that Gamla stood fast against the Romans, and the whole population participated in the war effort. In Jerusalem, in contrast, according to Josephus, the vast majority of the population was passive. The aristocracy was murdered by the Zealots and the Sicarii, while as soon as the siege began the lower strata of the population suffered from starvation. Those that dared to complain were murdered by the Zealots. In Masada the situation was different. The defenders of Masada consisted only of the Zealots and their families. Moreover their leader, Eleazar ben Yair, was probably a highly charismatic figure; the orders of the leaders were followed to the bitter end.

THE SITES AT WAR

This chapter presents a brief overview of siege warfare in Judaea between 168 BC and AD 73, with an emphasis on the Jewish War of AD 66–73. Once again, Josephus is the primary source of our knowledge of these events. It is important to stress that both the Hasmonaean and Herodian armies chiefly fought field battles, and were often the aggressors, meaning that most battles and sieges were conducted in enemy territory. The only sieges on home territory were the siege of Jerusalem by Pompey in 63 BC, which brought about the fall of the Hasmonaean dynasty, and Herod's siege of Jerusalem in 37 BC, which brought his line to power. It is thus ironic that many of the fortifications of Judaea – built or repaired by King Herod, probably one of the most faithful allies of Rome – were in fact used by the Jews in their struggle against Rome. Jotapata and Gamla in AD 67, Jerusalem in AD 70 and Masada in AD 72–73 were all examples of this, being besieged and taken by the Roman army.

It is a tribute to the architects and military engineers of the Hasmonaean and Herodian periods, as well as to the tenacity of the Jewish defenders, that these sieges are still remembered as among the toughest executed by the Roman army.

Pompey's siege of Jerusalem, 63 BC

In 66 BC, following the death of Queen Salome Alexandra, civil war broke out between her sons Hyrcanus II, the legitimate king and high priest, and Judah Aristobulus II. Hyrcanus was supported by Antipater the Idumaean, Herod's grandfather, and the neighbouring Nabataeans, while Aristobulus had the support of other elements including the army and the Sadducees. Hyrcanus besieged Aristobulus in Jerusalem with the help of the Nabataeans, and his army was later joined by a Roman army under Scaurus, sent by Pompey to Syria, which had recently fought in the Mitridatic Wars. Scaurus presented himself as a supporter of Hyrcanus, but he actually took bribes from both sides. Moreover, when Scaurus returned to Damascus, Aristobulus seized the opportunity to defeat Hyrcanus and his Nabataeans allies at the Battle of Papyron. However, when Pompey arrived in Syria both Hyrcanus and Aristobulus

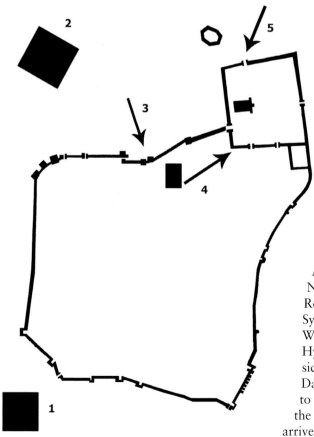

A plan of Pompey's siege of Jerusalem, 63 BC.
1 – first Roman camp,
2 – second Roman camp,
3 – the site where the Roman Army was let in by the supporters of Hyrcanus,
4/5 – the Roman attacks on the Temple Mount from the west and from the north. (Courtesy of Dalit Weinblatt–Krausz)

visited him in Damascus, attempting to settle the dispute in front of the Roman warlord. Pompey did not make any hasty promises, but he told the two Hasmonaean princes that he would settle the question on his arrival in Judaea. Aristobulus, however, did not wait for Pompey's judgment and fled to Judaea, shutting himself away in the fortress of Alexandrium. Pompey ordered Aristobulus to give up the fortress, but he refused. However, when Pompey reached Jericho, Aristobulus surrendered to him.

However, when Gabinius, sent by Pompey to take possession of Jerusalem, arrived at the gates of the city, he was shut out by Aristobulus's supporters. This time Pompey reacted angrily and had Aristobulus arrested. He also prepared to besiege Jerusalem. However, inside Jerusalem not all the population supported Aristobulus, and Pompey's army was let in by Hyrcanus's men, who opened a gate probably situated in the north-western part of the First Wall. Pompey thus became master of the city as well as of the Royal Palace. However, Aristobulus's supporters did not surrender, and instead holed themselves up in the area of the Temple Mount and of the City of David.

To reduce them, Pompey erected two camps; the first lay north-west of Jerusalem, and the second was situated to the south-west. He then created a ditch around the area where Aristobulus's supporters were entrenched, and

Herodian siege techniques

Our only evidence of Herodian siege techniques comes from Josephus's description of the events at Jerusalem in 37 BC (*Antiquities* XIV, 466). Josephus writes that Herod encompassed the city with three bulwarks, erected towers and cut down the trees that surrounded the city – reminiscent of the siege of Alesia by Julius Caesar in 52 BC. Clearly Herod's engineers followed a Roman deployment, not a Hellenistic one, which would have been characterized by the use of siege towers and catapults. It may well have been that Herod built only one ring of fortifications around Jerusalem, due to the remoteness of a relieving army coming to Antigonus's rescue.

It is also clear that Herod's army possessed artillery, both for siege warfare and to protect his own fortifications. Josephus writes that the fortification of Machaerous was 'stocked with abundance of weapons and engines' (*War* VII, 177). The Jewish patriots in the war against the Romans operated artillery machines from the fortifications of Jerusalem (*War* V, 267, 347, 358–59). These machines were probably mounted on the walls of Jerusalem in Herod's time, most likely comprising arrow- and stone-throwers, and were part of the standard equipment of the Late Hellenistic, late Republican and early imperial armies. In addition to Herod's siege-works and artillery probably following a Roman model, it seems likely that Roman engineers, or local engineers trained in Rome, served in Herod's army.

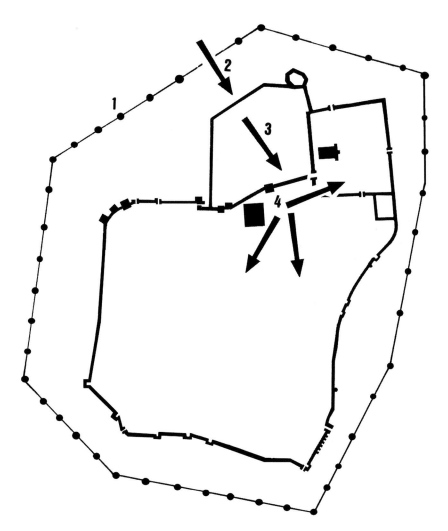

A plan of Herod's siege of Jerusalem, 37 BC. 1 – the siege wall of Herod's army, 2 – Herod's first attack, and conquest of the Second Wall, 3 – Herod's second attack and conquest of the First Wall, 4 – Herod's final attack, conquest of the Temple Mount, the Lower City, and the Upper City. (Courtesy of Dalit Weinblatt–Krausz)

erected two ramparts, the first north of the Bira fortress, filling in the valley, and the second west of the Temple Mount. Next Pompey brought up siege machines and battering rams from Tyre. Aristobulus's supporters would not fight against the besiegers on the Sabbath, the weekly holy day of rest for the Jews, but Pompey's army chose this for an attack. The Roman army, under the leadership of Cornelius Faustus Sulla, son of the well-known dictator, penetrated the city from the Bira fortress, while other attacks went in from the west, penetrating the Temple Mount and the northern part of the City of David. Very few Roman soldiers died during the siege, whereas some 12,000 Jewish defenders perished. Pompey himself entered the Holy of Holies of the Jewish Temple, where only the High Priest was permitted to tread, and desecrated it. The siege was a disaster for the Hasmoneans. The state was dismembered, and Hyrcanus retained only the title of High Priest, losing his royal title. His brother Aristobulus formed part of Pompey's triumphal procession in Rome.

Herod's siege of Jerusalem, 37 BC

In 40 BC the Parthians invaded Judaea. Hyrcanus II, high priest and ethnarch, was captured by the invaders and handed to his nephew Mattathias Antigonus, grandson of Aristobulus II. He had the nose and ears of the ageing Hyrcanus chopped off, thus putting an end to his tenure of the high priesthood. Herod, the son of Antipater the Idumaean, succeeded in fleeing to Rome. There the Roman Senate named Herod king of Judaea, following the suggestion of Antony and Octavian. Herod then returned to Judaea, where he faced Mattathias Antigonus and his supporters, although the Parthians, having been defeated by Antony's Romans, had retired.

First, Herod retook Galilee from Antigonus's supporters. Antony sent Ventidius, the governor of Syria, and Silo to Herod to help speed the campaign. However, Silo was corrupted by Antigonus, as were other successive Roman commanders sent by Antony to assist Herod. However, it would take Herod until the winter of 38/37 BC before he could trap Antigonus in Jerusalem. He was also smart enough to offers bigger bribes to the Roman officers than Antigonus, and to treat the Jewish population with clemency and sympathy.

Once Herod's army had advanced almost to Jerusalem, Antigonus had no choice other than to send out his regular army to face Herod in a pitched battle. Antigonus struck on two fronts; to the south he sent 6,000 soldiers to fight against the Roman allies encamped at Jericho, and in the north he sent his main army under his general Pappus against Machaerous in Samaria. Unfortunately for Antigonus, both forces were defeated. Herod took to the offensive against Pappus, and emerged victorious from the great pitched battle at the village of Isanas between the two sides.

After Herod's victory, Antigonus retired within Jerusalem. Herod's army pitched camp in front of the northern stretch of the First Wall of Jerusalem, but the arrival of winter ended military operations. In spring 37 BC Herod began his siege works. Following the dictates of Roman siege warfare, three concentric siege walls with towers were erected around the city. In the same period the reinforcements of Sosius, sent by Antony, arrived to support Herod's army. Herod's force numbered 30,000 men, and Sosius had collected together the strength of 11 legions, 6,000 cavalrymen and 6,000 auxiliaries from Syria. Much of the surrounding area lay fallow, making things difficult for the besieged in terms of provisions. The Roman–Herodian forces erected

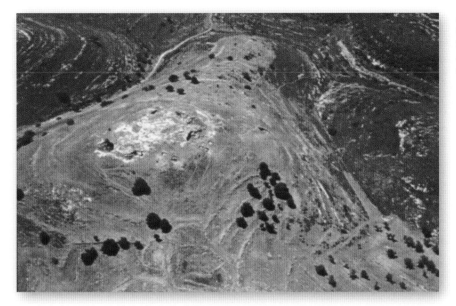

An aerial view of Jotapata. (Courtesy of Moti Aviam, Institute of Galilean Archaeology, University of Rochester)

siege towers and assembled battering rams, and dug galleries under the city walls. After 40 days, Herod's army breached what Josephus calls the 'north wall', which may have been the Second Wall, or an ad hoc fortification erected in advance of the siege by Antigonus. The First Wall fell 15 days later. It appears that Antigonus enclosed himself in the Baris fortress.

Herod's soldiers penetrated the Outer Temple Court, and during the ensuing battle the outer porticoes of the Temple were burnt down, probably by Antigonus's supporters. Only the Inner Court of the Temple and the Upper City still remained in Antigonus's hands. The Jewish defenders, besieged in the Inner Court of the Temple, begged Herod to allow the passage of animals and other offerings to continue the Temple sacrifice, a request with which Herod complied in order not to lose popularity. However, after fruitless negotiation, Herod decided to storm the rest of the city. Once taken, the Roman soldiers showed no restraint, and Herod was forced to complain to Antony about their behaviour. Antigonus gave himself up to Sosius, who handed him to Antony. The fate of the unhappy Hasmonaean prince was sealed, and he was beheaded. Herod was now master of his kingdom.

The siege of Jotapata, AD 67

In AD 66 the Jewish rebellion against Rome broke out in Jerusalem. Gessius Florus, the Roman governor of Judaea, was forced to abandon Jerusalem and fled to Caesarea Maritima. The new government of the Jewish patriots, formed by the most important and respected members of the Jewish priestly aristocracy, often identified with the Sadducees, still wished peace and tried to avoid a definite break with Rome. However, Cestius Gallus, the governor of Roman Syria, organized an expedition against Jerusalem, and he was defeated by the Jewish patriots at the Battle of Beth Horon. The battle brought a rebellion inside Agrippa II's kingdom in Galilee. Some cities, such as the capital of the kingdom Tiberias, took the side of the rebels, while others, such as Sepphoris, remained neutral. The rebellion then extended from Galilee to the northern part of Agrippa II's territories and the Golan.

Meanwhile, in Jerusalem the new government gave command of Galilee to the young Joseph ben Mattitiyahu. However, the moderate, aristocratic leadership of priestly stock was soon challenged by the extremist Zealots and Sicarii. As a result, Joseph ben Mattitiyahu's efforts to transform the Jews from an armed rabble into an organized army failed miserably, hampered by the demagogue Yochanan of Gush Halav. Joseph ben Mattitiyahu had to change his strategy, and began to fortify the cities of Galilee.

The emperor Nero called on Vespasian, who had already distinguished himself during Claudius's conquest of Britannia, to quell the rebellion. In AD 67 Vespasian arrived in Antioch and began to organize a Roman army, consisting of the V Legio Macedonica, the X Legio Fretensis, 23 cohorts of auxiliary infantry, six wings of auxiliary cavalry, and the armies of the client kings Agrippa II (who remained faithful to Rome), Antiochus of Commagene, Soaemus of Emesa, and Malichus II of Nabataea – a total of around 60,000 soldiers. Vespasian's army was joined at Ptolemais by his son Titus and the XV Legio Apollinaris coming from Alexandria. Vespasian's strategy was first to reduce Galilee and then the rest of Agrippa's kingdom. By this stage Joseph ben Mattitiyahu had fortified the most important towns of Galilee. The Jews faced Vespasian's army at Garis, near Sepphoris, and were defeated. As a consequence Sepphoris, which had adopted a neutral stance, opened its gates to the Romans.

Joseph ben Mattitiyahu retired to Tiberias, and then shut himself inside the small fortified city of Jotapata. On hearing this, Vespasian sent 1,000 cavalryman to seal off the town. Then the whole Roman army followed and set camp around the city. Although it had a small surface area, Jotapata was very difficult to assault, and could be approached only from the top of a hill facing the city. Vespasian began the siege with his artillery, backed by the lightly armed troops, who rained down a constant stream of projectiles on the defenders. Meanwhile, the Romans erected a ramp to reach the level of the city's battlements, forcing Joseph ben Mattitiyahu to order the height of the city walls to be raised.

Having completed the ramp, the Romans began to batter the walls of the city with a ram. The defenders succeeded in breaking off the ram's head with a boulder thrown from the walls, and set fire to it. However, by the same evening the Romans had already repaired the ram. At dawn the next day the city wall collapsed, but the Roman soldiers were driven off by the city defenders. To spare his soldiers' lives, Vespasian erected siege towers covered in iron, which were set near the walls to keep the defenders under fire. The Romans heightened the ramp until it surpassed the city battlements and, after 47 days of siege, penetrated the city. It was razed to the ground, and around 40,000 Jews were killed.

Joseph ben Mattitiyahu hid himself in an underground cave with 40 fellow defenders; although he wished to surrender, the others refused. What happened then is not clear. It seems that the vast majority of the defenders opted to kill themselves rather than fall into the hands of the Romans. However, Joseph ben Mattitiyahu survived this last ordeal and surrendered to the Romans. According to his writings, Joseph ben Mattitiyahu prophesied to Vespasian that he would soon become emperor. Whatever actually happened, the Roman general spared his life and Joseph began to collaborate with the Roman army. By the end of the war, he was freed, given Roman citizenship with the name of Flavius Joseph and was elevated to the equestrian rank. While some consider him a coward, his behaviour in the last days of the siege of Jotapata resulted in the survival of one of the best historians of antiquity.

The siege of Gamla, AD 67

After the fall of Jotapata, Tiberias surrendered to Agrippa I, and Titus conquered the fortress of Tarichae after a brief siege. Only Gush Halav and Har Tavor were besieged by the Romans, the rest of Galilee being in Roman hands, save for the fortress of Gamla, which dominated the road from the Golan to Galilee and still offered resistance. Vespasian thus moved to the Golan, and began a siege of the site.

The siege developed in four distinct phases. At first the legionaries of the Legio V attacked from the north-east in two spots, near the towers and near the synagogue. After a fierce battle they managed to breach the wall using a battering ram. The second phase began when the Romans broke in; they were forced to fight an uphill battle in the narrow streets and alleys, near the northern wall. The Romans were unable to manoeuvre because their comrades were crowding behind them, and many legionaries climbed on the roofs of the houses that were built in terraces up the hillside. Under their weight the houses collapsed on top of each other, and many Romans died buried in the rubble or choked to death on the dust. The defenders counter-attacked, causing panic among the Romans and forcing them to retreat. The third phase started some days later, when the legionaries of the Legio XV attacked from the north-west during the night, at the intersection of the southern wall and the cliff to the west. They dislodged some of the stones at the base of the large tower, which collapsed. The following morning the Romans re-entered the town, and once more bitter street fighting took place, until the Romans eventually reached the lofty citadel. The last phase consisted of the capture of this feature. These defenders not killed by the Romans threw themselves from the citadel walls. Only two women survived the battle.

After the conquest of Gamla, Gush Halav surrendered to Titus and Har Tavor was taken too. In Jerusalem the loss of Galilee led to civil war between the priestly ruling class and the Zealots, the latter calling on the Idumaeans to aid them in their cause. Once Agrippa's kingdom had been secured, Vespasian moved to Peraea and the Decapolis, where the Gentile cities of Gadara and Gerasa, which were in Jewish hands, were conquered. Vespasian then moved to Judaea, where he took the cities of Lydda, Emmaus and Yamnia. By AD 67 Peraea, the Decapolis and Judaea were in Roman hands, and Jerusalem, Masada, Herodium and a few other fortresses, as well as Idumea, were alone in resisting the Roman onslaught.

A plan of Gamla, AD 67.
1 – outer wall, 2 – Twin Tower Gate, 3 – Round Tower, 4 – public building (synagogue), 5 – Summit Tower.

0   50   100

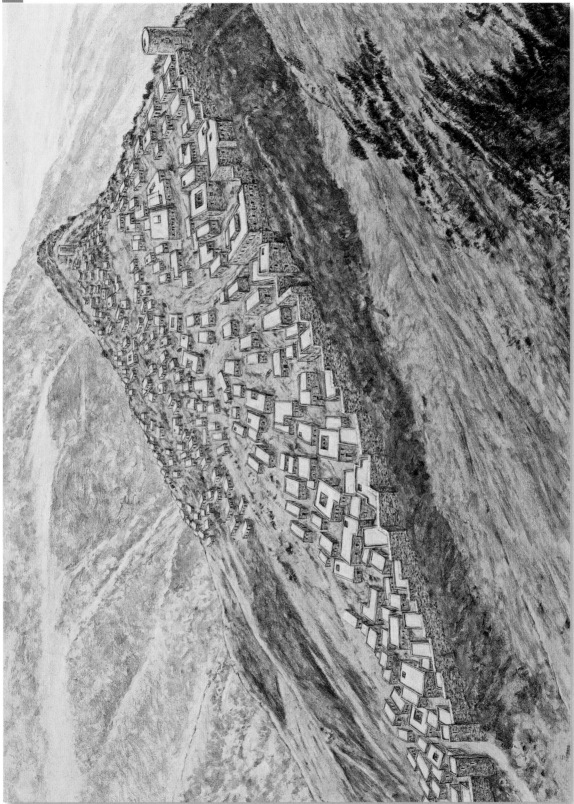

The siege of Jerusalem, AD 69–70

In AD 68, following the conquest of Galilee, Vespasian brought his army back to Caesarea. There he learnt that Nero had committed suicide and that Galba had become emperor. Vespasian now began the conquest of Judaea itself. Gophna and Acrabata in Judaea were swiftly taken, as was Hebron in Idumaea. In AD 69 Galba was murdered by the Praetorians, who favoured Otho for the imperial seat; the western legions, on the other hand, proclaimed Vitellius emperor, and the two sides clashed at Cremona, resulting in Otho's defeat and eventual suicide. To complicate matters, the eastern legion proclaimed Vespasian emperor, leading him to leave Judaea for Alexandria and then Rome. His son Titus was given supreme command of the war in Judaea, while Vespasian's forces under Antonius Primus defeated Vitellius's army at Cremona.

Meanwhile, in Jerusalem interfactional fighting broke out between the various groups of Zealots. Yochanan of Gush Halav's leadership was challenged by Shimon Bar Giora, and the new high priest sided with him. Moreover a new faction, under the leadership of Eleazar ben Shimon, was organized in Jerusalem. Each group controlled a different part of the city: Yochanan the Temple Mount, Shimon the Upper City, and Eleazar the Temple itself. When a group of pilgrims arrived at the Temple, Yochanan seized the opportunity to wipe out Eleazar's faction. This savage civil war destroyed many of the city's stores and provisions, condemning the besieged city to its fate. Yochanan and Shimon decided, too late, to coordinate their efforts in the defence of Jerusalem.

Titus began the siege of Jerusalem with four legions, the V, X, XII and XV and an equivalent number of auxiliary units. The Roman army erected two camps on Mount Scopus (V, XII, XV legions) and on the Mount of Olives (X Legion). The Jews repeatedly attacked the Roman army and their camps, but without result. Later on, the V, XII and XV legions were moved to a second and a third camp, the first facing the Third Wall from the north-west, and the second facing the north-west side of the Second Wall, in front of the Citadel and Herod's Palace. The Jewish defenders numbered around 23,000; Simon had 10,000 followers, plus 5,000 Idumaeans, who managed the northern and western defences. John had 8,400 Zealots under him, which included the men who were once followers of Eleazar's party, and these held the eastern defences.

A plan of Titus's siege of Jerusalem, AD 70. 1 – Roman main camp on Mount Scopus, 2 – Roman camp on the Mount of Olives, 3 – third Roman camp, facing the city from the north-west, 4 – fourth Roman camp facing the Citadel, 5 – Roman breach in the Third Wall, 6 – Roman camp in the area of the New City, 7 – Roman breach in the Second Wall, 8 – Roman attack on the Antonia; note that Titus's circumvallation wall is shown with a dotted line, 9 – Roman attack on the Temple Mount, 10 – final Roman attack, breach in the First Wall and conquest of the Lower City.

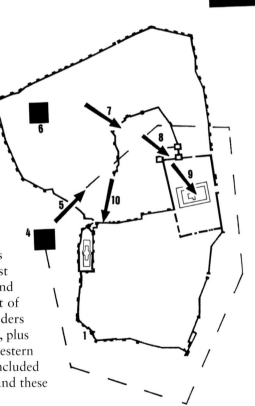

Titus attacked the Third Wall from the north-west with the V, XII and XV legions. The wall was breached and the Romans quickly mastered the New City, defended by the Third Wall. Titus decided to exploit the impetus of his soldiers and continued the attack on the Second Wall. Five days after the fall of the Third Wall, the Second Wall was also taken. At this point Titus divided his army. Two legions were given the order to attack the city defended by the First Wall, while two more were sent to attack the Temple area. The Romans attacked the Antonia fortress, piling up earth around its sides, and pushing the siege machines near the fortress walls. This time, however, the impetus of the Roman attack faltered, and the defenders destroyed the siege machines. Titus then asked for a truce. When the Jewish defenders refused to surrender, Titus understood that he was in for a long siege.

The Romans next erected a wall of circumvallation around the First Wall, the Temple Mount and the Antonia fortress. Moreover, the V, XII and XV legions were moved to a third camp inside the area of the New City. Titus then began the final attack on Jerusalem. The Romans filled the ditches around the Antonia fortress, and covered them with wooden structures. The Jewish defenders attacked these works but were repulsed. Then the Romans began to batter down the outer wall of the Antonia. The wall collapsed, partly due to the mines dug by the defenders in their efforts to destroy the Roman works. However, the Romans had to face another inner wall, prepared by the defenders in case the outer wall fell. For two days the Romans fought to take this wall; during the night a small group of soldiers scaled the walls and killed the guards, and the subsequent attack took the wall. The Jews, thinking that the Romans were already masters of the Antonia, fled, leaving the fortress in the hands of the Romans. Titus destroyed all of it, save for the platform, on which he would be able to bring his siege machines up to the outer wall of the Temple.

The Romans then attacked the Temple Courts defended by Shimon Bar Giora, which resisted for five more weeks, before burning down Herod's Temple. Shimon Bar Giora retreated behind the First Wall, and a month later this and the rest of the city fell. The Romans burned everything to the ground, save the three towers of the citadel, which Titus ordered spared as a testimony to the former might of Jerusalem. The siege of Jerusalem had lasted six months. Both Yochanan of Gush Halav and Shimon Bar Giora were captured, and exhibited during Titus's triumphal procession in Rome. After the procession, Shimon Bar Giora was beheaded.

The siege of Masada, AD 72–73

With the conquest of Jerusalem in the summer of AD 70, Jewish resistance had all but ended. On the fringes of Judaea, however, a minority of Jewish patriots refused to surrender to the Romans, even after the destruction of the Temple and Jerusalem.

Following Titus's return to Rome, a new governor, Flavius Silva, of senatorial rank, took control of Judaea and the Roman army there in AD 72. The main challenge he faced was from a 960-strong group of Sicarii (which included women and children) under the leadership of Eleazar ben Yair, which held the fortress of Masada near the Dead Sea. Silva gathered the X Legio Fretensis, plus six cohorts of auxiliaries, and prepared to besiege the fortress.

The siege took place in the winter of AD 72–73. The Romans first diverted the aqueducts of the fortress for their own use. Then they erected a circumvallatory wall around Masada. This wall, built using local stone, was reinforced by towers, erected on the western side, and by military camps planned as part of the siege barrier. Thus, half of the legion (cohorts VI–X) was encamped on the low ground, east of the fortress, and the other half (cohorts I–V) was encamped on the higher ground to the west, where Silva established his headquarters. The auxiliary cohorts were camped in six other locations.

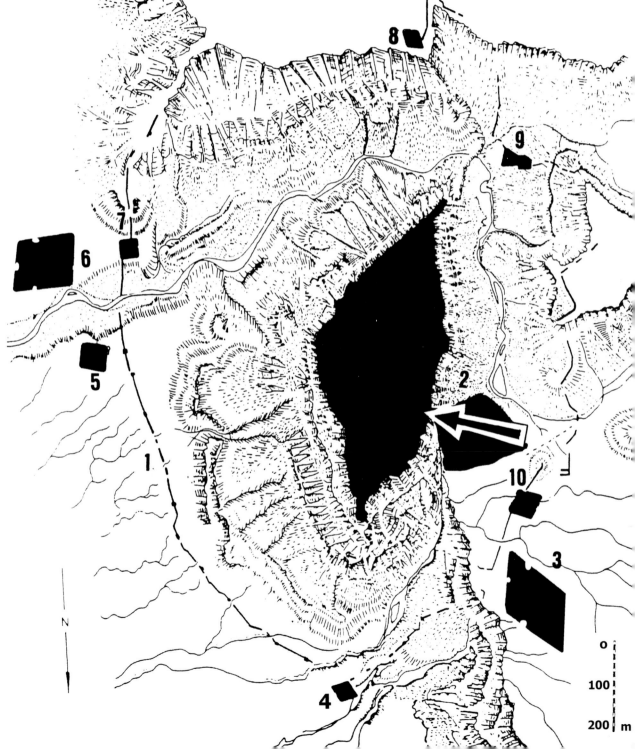

A plan of Flavius Silva's siege of Masada AD 72/73. 1 – Roman wall of circumvallation, 2 – Roman ramp, 3 – main Roman camp of cohorts I–V, 6 – camp of cohorts VI–X; 4, 5, and 7 – auxiliary camps on the east side of the wall of circumvallation; 8, 9 and 10 – auxiliary camps on the west side of the wall of circumvallation.

1. Northern Palace
2. Storehouse complex
3. Governor's Palace
4. Bathhouse
5. Western Palace
6. Snake Path Gate
7. Stables (later, the synagogue)
8. Cisterns
9. Columbarium
10. Casemate wall
11. Southern fort

Once Masada had been isolated from the surrounding area, the Romans built a ramp on the west side of the fortress, a common practice of Roman military engineers. This ramp had a 20-degree incline, and was built (by Jewish prisoners) using a frame of timber layers covered with earth. Once the ramp was ready, the Romans built a siege tower with a battering ram on the front. This siege tower had special features; as the ramp was quite steep, the siege tower was built following the same angle of the slope. Once the Romans had brought the siege tower near to the wall of the fortress, the battering ram began to break it down. However, the Sicarii quickly erected an inner wall made of earth and timber, the latter probably taken from the roofs of Herod's palaces.

The more the Romans battered the wall, the more compacted the earth became, forcing them to change their tactics. They opted to set fire to the inner wall, hoping to burn down its timber frame, but the wind blew the fire back onto the siege tower, setting it alight. Later, however, the wind changed direction and the inner wall erected by the Sicarii caught fire. The Romans were now ready to attack the fortress, but it was not to be. Eleazar ben Yair called an assembly of his followers, probably inside a building adjacent to the western wall that had been transformed into a synagogue. There he persuaded them that it was better to commit suicide as free men than to fall into the hands of the Romans and be enslaved. The Sicarii committed suicide together with their families. The following morning the Romans found only two old women and two children alive, who recounted what had happened. The Jewish War was now well and truly over.

AFTERMATH

By the end of AD 73, with the exception of most of the Gentile cities, such as Caesarea Maritima and Sebaste, and the Greek cities, most notably Skythopolis, Judaea lay in ruins. The first step taken by the Flavian dynasty in Rome was to establish colonies in Judaea to control their Jewish subjects. Nero had already established the colony of Akko-Ptolemais. On its coins are depicted the standards of the legions III Gallica, VI Ferrata, X Fretensis and XII Fulminata. Vespasian established a colony at Caesarea Maritima, the Colonia Prima Flavia Augusta Caesarea. Later, Domitian established another Roman colony at Flavia Neapolis, modern Schechem. Flavian Judaea became a senatorial province, and was no longer an equestrian one, a move intended to prevent the abuses that brought the Jews to revolt in AD 66. Jerusalem was left in ruins, although the X Legion Fretensis remained there, encamped on the site of Herod's Palace, protected by the three surviving towers of the citadel. Jews, however, continued to live in the area around Jerusalem. Galilee was returned to the ageing Agrippa II, who died probably in AD 98. With the death of Agrippa, the last Herodian ruler, Trajan annexed Galilee to the empire. Moreover in AD 106, he annexed the neighbouring Nabataean kingdom, creating the Provincia Arabia.

The Jews would once more fight against the Romans, under the leadership of Bar Kochba from AD 132–35, in Hadrian's reign. The latter wished to rebuild Jerusalem as a Roman colony, Aelia Capitolina, and to erect a temple dedicated to Jupiter Capitolinus on the site of the Jewish Temple. After three years of a hard-fought and bloody guerrilla war, mainly in southern Judaea, the Romans crushed the revolt. The results were even more demoralizing for the Jews than the First War. Judaea was completely emptied of its Jewish population. Moreover, Hadrian changed the name of the province from Judaea to Syria-Palaestina to erase the name of the Jews from the map. It seems that the ruins of the Herodium were utilized as a military base by the Jewish rebels, although by then not one of the Hasmonaean and Herodian forts considered in this book were in use, either by the Romans or by the rebels.

Hadrian rebuilt Jerusalem as the Roman colony Aelia Capitolina, where the Legion X Fretensis continued to reside. In Galilee at Legio, a permanent military camp for the Legion VI Macedonica was erected. However, the capital of Syria-Palaestina was still Caesarea Maritima, which continued to develop during the 2nd century AD, as an aqueduct erected in Hadrian's day testifies. By then, however, the Herodian city walls were no longer in use. The Jewish population was by then mainly concentrated in Galilee. It seems that the Jews of Galilee did not take part in the Bar Kochba war, and that as a consquence prosperity in the countryside of Galilee had returned by the middle of the 2nd century.

Moreover, the most important urban centres of Galilee had survived intact. Tiberias was only lightly damaged by the war in AD 67, and together with Sepphoris both cities continued to develop in the 2nd and 3rd centuries AD, mainly as Jewish cities. The well-known Jewish patriarch, Rabbi Yehuda Ha Nasi, the Prince, lived in Sepphoris. He was on very friendly terms with the Roman administration and probably the imperial house as well. Tiberias actually had become a Roman colony by the time of the emperor Elagabalus (r. AD 218–22), this time as an honour and not a punishment. In roughly the same period the Herodian foundation of Samaria became a colony under Septimius Severus (AD 201), called Colonia Lucia Septimia Sebaste. Later Jewish patriarchs in the 3rd–5th centuries continued to live in Tiberias.

A reconstruction of the Herodian Temple Mount. On the right the Royal Stoa can be seen. In the centre stands the Temple. (The Jerusalem Model, courtesy of the Holyland Hotel)

The emperor Diocletian (r. AD 284–305) divided the province of Syria-Palaestina into three smaller provinces, Palaestina Prima, Palaestina Secunda, and Palaestina Tertia at the end of the 3rd century AD. By the middle of the 4th century AD, the area was feeling the effects of slow but increasing Christianization; Aelia Capitolina was transformed into the Christian city of Hierosolyma, with the erection of various churches, the most important being the Holy Sepulchre. In the late Roman period new fortifications and city walls were erected everywhere, including in the Holy Land. By then, most of the Hasmonaean and the Herodian fortifications were long forgotten.

THE SITES TODAY

The Hasmonean and Herodian fortifications were widely excavated in the 20th century. Jerusalem was, and still is, the most interesting and important archaeological site in Israel. The earliest excavations of the fortifications of Herodian Jerusalem were conducted by Professor L.A. Mayer, who excavated the Third Wall in the late 1920s. However, Second Temple-period Jerusalem was excavated mostly after the Six Day War. Professor Mazar excavated at the foot of the Temple Mount, while Professor Avigad, assisted by Reich and Geva, excavated the Jewish Quarter. Further excavations were directed by Dan Bahat in the Citadel.

Caesarea Maritima has a long history of archaeological research. The first relevant excavations were directed by Professor A. Frova of the University of Milan. Today various universities, including Haifa University (under the direction of A. Raban, who has excavated the harbour structures) and the University of Maryland (under the direction of K. Holum), as well as the Israel Antiquity Authority (under the direction of J. Patrich) are conducting excavations. A few years ago the late Professor Hirschfeld excavated the complex of Ramat Ha Nadiv, which includes the fortress of Horvat 'Eleq.

One of the most important sites is, of course, Masada, which has become an important symbol in Israeli consciousness; today, recruits from the Israel Defence Forces swear their oath of loyalty to the State of Israel at Masada, with the words 'Masada will not fall again!' Yadin excavated Masada in the 1960s, and today the whole site has been restored and is a World Heritage site protected by UNESCO. The palace-fortress at Herodium has been excavated twice, notably by Professor Netzer of the Hebrew University of Jerusalem. In Galilee, Gamla has been excavated by Shemariahu Gutnmann assisted by D. Syon. Yotapata/Jutfat has been excavated by M. Aviam.

For those who wish to visit the Hasmonaean and Herodian fortresses, the best place to start is in Jerusalem. The model of Jerusalem in the Second Temple period at the Israel Museum (www.imj.org.il) provides an excellent beginning. Moreover, various artefacts connected to the Hasmonaeans, Herod and the First Revolt can be seen in the permanent exhibition there, together with the Dead Sea Scrolls. The Old City of Jerusalem is also important. The Tower of David Museum (www.towerofdavid.org.il) located in the Ottoman citadel is dedicated to the history of Jerusalem through the ages. A sizeable part of the exhibition is dedicated to the development of Jerusalem in the Hasmonaean and Herodian periods. One of the towers of the Ottoman citadel is one of the three Herod built, most probably the Phaseael Tower. In the Jewish Quarter it is possible to visit the Wohl Archaeological Museum of Jerusalem as well as the Burnt House. These are two Herodian mansions that were burned down in AD 70. From the Byzantine *cardo*, at the end of the covered mall, it is also possible to reach the remains of a Hasmonaean tower, part of the northern stretch of the First Wall.

Israel is a small country, and so most of the sites can easily be reached from Jerusalem. The Herodion National Park is situated midway along the road from Jerusalem to Bethlehem. Masada National Park is situated near the Dead Sea. To reach this symbolic site, it is necessary to pass via Qumran, where the Dead Sea Scrolls were probably written. Caesarea National Park, located on the coast, is very near to the city of Natanya, with easy access from the coastal highway. It is also worthwhile to visit the Sdoth Yam Museum, with its collection of Roman antiquities from Caesarea. Not far from Caesarea, in the small city of Zikron Yakov the Park of Ramat Ha Nadiv is located, in which lies the fortress of Horvat 'Eleq. In northern Galilee the most important sites are Tiberias, where it is possible to see the remains of the Antipas Gate not far from the southern stretch of the Ottoman walls of the city, and Gamla. From Tiberias one can reach the Gamla National Park on the Golan Plateau. However, one should bear in mind that Gamla itself is a 1½-hour walk away. More can be learnt about all the National Parks (Massada, Gamla, Herodion and Caesarea) via the website of the Israel Nature and National Park Protection Authority (www.parks.org.il).

CHRONOLOGY

Hasmonaean period (168–40 BC)

168 BC Beginning of the Maccabaean rebellion against Seleucid rule.

164 BC Judah Maccabaeus enters Jerusalem and reconsecrates the Temple.

161 BC Judah Maccabaeus is victorious at Hadasa over Nicanor. Bacchides defeats Judah Maccabaeus at Elasa.

161–143 BC Jonathan the Hasmonaean is appointed high priest and *strategos* (military leader) by Alexander Balas, a Seleucid usurper.

143–135 BC Simon is appointed ethnarch of Judaea and high priest by Demetrius II.

135–107 BC John Hyrcanus I is appointed ethnarch and high priest. He conquers Idumaea, parts of Galilee and Samaria.

104–103 BC Judah Aristobulus I is king and high priest.

101–76 BC Alexander Jannaeus is king and high priest. He conquers the coastal cities of Dora and Gaza, and most of the Decapolis and the Hauran regions in Transjordan.

76–66 BC Queen Salome Alexandra rules.

66–63 BC Civil war between Hyrcanus II, supported by Antipater the Idumaean, and Aristobulus II. The two brothers call in Pompey to settle the dispute.

63 BC Pompey besieges and defeats Aristobulus II at Jerusalem. Hyrcanus II is appointed high priest. The Hasmonaean kingdom is broken up.

48 BC Hyrcanus II and Antipater side with Caesar after the Battle of Pharsalus.

47 BC Caesar bestows on Hyrcanus II the titles of ethnarch and 'ally of Rome'.

44–42 BC Antipater is murdered. Herod succeeds his father.

Herodian period (40–4 BC)

40 BC The Parthians invade Roman Syria and Judaea. Herod is appointed king of Judaea in Rome.

39–37 BC Herod conquers Judaea.

32 BC First Nabataean War.

31 BC After the Battle of Actium, Herod sides with Octavian.

30 BC At Rhodes Herod is confirmed king of Judaea by Octavian.

25 BC Samaria is rebuilt as Sebaste in honour of Augustus.

23–22 BC Herod is given Trachonitis, Batanaea and Auranitis by Augustus.

20 BC Augustus presents Herod with the territory of Zenodorus in Ituraea.

20–19 BC Herod begins the rebuilding of the Temple in Jerusalem.

15 BC Agrippa visits Herod in Jerusalem. The Temple is dedicated.

10 BC Dedication of Caesarea Maritima.

9 BC Second Nabataean War. Herod is, for a while, out of favour with Augustus.

4 BC On Herod's death, his kingdom is divided between his three sons Archelaus (4 BC–AD 6) ethnarch of Judaea, Samaria and Idumaea; Antipas (4 BC–AD 39) tetrarch of Galilee; and Philip (4 BC–AD 33) tetrarch of Gaulanitis, Hauranitis and Batanaea.

Roman rule (AD 6–66)

AD **6**   Augustus annexes the territories of Archelaus to the Roman province of Syria. Judaea is ruled by a *praefectus*, the best-known of whom is Pontius Pilatus.

AD **41**   Claudius makes Agrippa king of Judaea.

AD **44**   Claudius annexes the whole of Judaea, which is ruled by a procurator.

AD **44–66**   The political and social situation deteriorates. Rise of the Zealots and Sicarii.

The Jewish War (AD 66–70)

AD **66**   Beginning of the rebellion in Jerusalem. Gessius Florus, the Roman procurator, flees to Caesarea. The army of Cestius Gallus, the governor of Syria, is defeated by the rebels at Beth Horon. Rebellion of Galilee against Agrippa II.

AD **67**   Vespasian conquers Galilee. At the siege of Jotapata, Joseph ben Mattitiyahu surrenders to the Romans. Vespasian moves to the Golan. Siege and conquest of Gamla. Gush Halav surrenders to Titus. In Jerusalem the loss of Galilee causes a civil war between the rebel government and the Zealots. By the end of the year Vespasian has conquered Peraea, Decapolis and most of Judaea, with the exception of Jerusalem.

AD **69**   The Eastern Legion proclaims Vespasian emperor; he leaves Judaea for Rome. Titus begins the siege of Jerusalem. In Jerusalem civil war erupts between the various groups of Zealots.

AD **70**   Jerusalem is stormed, and the city and the Temple are destroyed. The Zealot leaders Yochanan of Gush Halav and Shimon Bar Giora are taken prisoner.

AD **73**   Flavius Silva, the newly appointed governor of Judaea, conquers Masada. The Zealots and their families, under the leadership of Eleazar ben Yair, elect to commit suicide rather than to fall into Roman hands.

FURTHER READING

Abbreviations

BAR   *British Archaeological Reports*

BASOR *Bulletin of American Schools of Oriental Research*

IEJ   *Israel Exploration Journal*

LA   *Liber Annus*

PEQ   *Palestine Exploration Quarterly*

Arav, R., *Settlement patterns and city planning, 337–301 B.C.E.*, British Archaeological Reports, International Series 485 (Oxford, 1989)

Aharoni, Y. and R. Amiran, 'Excavations at Tel Arad, Preliminary Report on the First Season, 1962', *IEJ* 14, 1964, pp. 131–47

Aharoni, Y., 'Tel Beersheba', *IEJ* 24, 1974, p. 271

Ariel, D. T., 'Tel Istaba', *IEJ* 38, 1988, pp. 30–35

Arnould, C., 'Les arcs romains de Jérusalem', *Novum Testamentum et Orbis Antiquus* 35 (Fribourg, 1997)

Aviam, M., 'Yodefat/Jotapata: The Archaeology of the First Battle', in Berlin, A. M. and Overman, J. A. (eds.), *The First Jewish Revolt: Archaeology, History, and Ideology*, pp. 121–33 (London, 2002)

Bahat, D., *The Illustrated Atlas of Jerusalem* (Jerusalem, 1990)

Barag, D., 'King Herod's Royal Castle at Samaria–Sebaste', *PEQ* 125, 1993, pp. 3–17

Barag, D. et al, *Masada IV: The Yigael Yadin Excavations 1963-1965, Final Reports, Lamps, Textiles, Basketry, Cordage and Related Artifacts, Wood Remains, Ballista Balls* (Jerusalem, 1995)

Bar-Kochva, B., *Judah Maccabaeus. The Jewish Struggle against the Seleucids* (Cambridge, 1989)

Beit-Arieh, I., 'Tel 'Ira: A Stronghold in the Biblical Negev', Tel Aviv University, Institute of Archaeology, Monograph Series No. 15 (Tel Aviv, 1999)

Ben-Arieh, S., 'The "Third Wall" of Jerusalem', in Yadin, Y. (ed.), *Ancient Jerusalem Revealed, Archaeology in the Holy City 1968–1974*, pp. 60–63 (Jerusalem, 1976)

Biran, A. and A. Cohen, 'Aroer in the Negev', *Eretz-Israel* 15, 1981, pp. 250–73

Connolly, P., *The Roman Army* (London, 1976)

Connolly, P., *Living in the Time of Jesus Christ* (Oxford, 1983)

Cotton, H. M. and J. Geiger, *Masada II: The Yigael Yadin Excavations 1963–1965, Final Reports, The Latin and Greek Documents*, (Jerusalem, 1989)

Corbo, V., 'Macheronte, La regia fortezza erodiana', *LA* 29, 1979, pp. 315–26

Crowfoot, J. W., *The Buildings at Samaria* (London, 1942)

Dar, S., *Landscape and Pattern. An Archaeological Survey of Samaria, 800 B.C.E. – 636 C.E.* (Debevoise, NC, 1986)

Eshel, E., and Z. E. Erlich, 'The Fortress of Acraba in Kh. Urmeh', *Cathedra* 47, 1988, pp. 17–24

Foerster, G., *Masada V: The Yigael Yadin Excavations 1963–1965, Final Reports, Art and Architecture* (Jerusalem, 1995)

Frova, A., *Scavi di Caesarea Maritima* (Milan, 1965)

Funk, R. W., 'The 1957 Campaign at Beth-Zur', *BASOR* 150, 1958, pp. 8–20

Gichon, M., 'Idumaea and the Herodian Limes', *IEJ* 17, 1967, pp. 27–42

Gracey, H. M., 'The Armies of the Judaean Client Kings', in Freeman, P. and D. Kennedy (eds.), *The Defence of the Roman and Byzantine East: Proceedings of a Colloquium Held at the University of Sheffield in April 1986*, BAR International Series 295 (Oxford, 1986)

Hirschfeld, Y., 'The Early Roman Bath and Fortress at Ramat Hanadiv near Caesarea', in *The Roman and Byzantine Near East: Some Recent Archaeological Research*, Journal of Roman Archaeology Supplementary Series No. 14, 1995, pp. 28–54

Hirschfeld, Y., *Ramat Hanadiv Excavations, Final Report of the 1984–1998 Seasons*, (Jerusalem, 2000)

Holum, K. G., *King Herod's Dream, Caesarea on the Sea* (New York, 1988)

Horowitz, J., 'Town Planning of Hellenistic Marisa', *PEQ* 112, 1980, pp. 93–111

Magen, M., 'Excavations at the Damascus Gate', in *Ancient Jerusalem Revealed*, pp. 281–87 (Jerusalem, 2000)

Marsden, E. W., *Greek and Roman Artillery: Historical Development* (Oxford, 1969)

Mayer, L. A., *The Third Wall of Jerusalem: An Account of Excavations* (Jerusalem, 1930)

Netzer, E., 'Cypros', *Qadmoniot* 8, 1975, pp. 54–61

Netzer, E., 'Greater Herodium', *Qedem* 13, 1981

Netzer, E., *Masada III: The Yigael Yadin Excavations 1963–1965, Final Reports, The Buildings, Stratigraphy and Architecture* (Jerusalem, 1991)

Netzer, E., *The Palaces of the Hasmoneans and Herod the Great* (Mainz, 1999)

Nielsen, I., *Hellenistic Palaces, Tradition and Renewal* (Aahrus, 1994)

Richardson, P., *Herod, King of the Jews and Friend of the Romans* (Columbia, SC, 1996)

Schalit, A., *König Herodes, Der Mann und sein Werk* (Berlin, 1969)

Schürer, E., *The History of the Jewish People in the Age of Jesus Christ (175 B.C.E –A.D. 135) I* (Edinburgh, 1973)

Sellers, O. R., *The Citadel of Beth Zur* (Philadelphia, 1933)

Shatzman, I., 'The Armies of the Hasmonaeans and Herod', *Texte und Studien zum Antiken Judentum* 25, 1991

Stern, E., 'The Walls of Dor', *IEJ* 38, 1988, pp. 6–14

Stern, E., *Dor Ruler of the Seas* (Jerusalem, 1994)

Syon, D., 'Gamla: City of Refuge', in Berlin, A. M. and J. A. Overman (eds.), *The First Jewish Revolt, Archaeology, History, and Ideology*, pp. 134–55 (London, 2002)

Talmon, T. and Y. Yigael, *Masada VI: The Yigael Yadin Excavations 1963–1965, Final Reports, Hebrew Fragments from Masada, The Ben Sira Scroll from Masada*, with notes on the reading by E. Qimron and bibliography by F. Garcia Martinez (Jerusalem, 1999)

Tsafrir, Y., and Y. Magen, 'The Desert Fortresses of Judaea in the Second Temple Period', *The Jerusalem Cathedra* 2, 1982, pp. 120–45

Tsafrir, Y., and Y. Magen, 'Two Seasons of Excavations at the Sartaba–Alexandrium Fortress', *Qadmoniot* 17, 1984, pp. 26–32

Wright, G. R. H., 'The Archaeological Remains at El-Mird in the Wilderness of Judaea', *Biblica* 42, 1961, pp. 1–21

Yadin, Y., J. Naveh and Y. Meshorer, *Masada I: The Yigael Yadin Excavations 1963–1965, Final Reports, The Aramaic and Hebrew Ostraca and Jar Inscriptions* (Jerusalem, 1989)

GLOSSARY

Ashlar	Stone cut into rectangular blocks and laid in regular rows.
Bastions	Wide sections of the city wall. Unlike towers, bastions did not often rise above the wall.
Casemate wall	A wall consisting of two parallel walls, the inner being thinner, which were divided by parallel walls into chambers. These were generally used for storage.
Crennellation	The alternating high and low sections of stonework along the top of a defensive wall. The defenders were protected behind the high section while firing their weapons in the openings over the lower sections.
Gradient	Sloping land.
Headers	Ashlar stones laid in a wall, according to its width.
Katoikos	Military colonist in Ancient Greece and in the Hellenistic east.
Kleros	An allotment of land distributed to military colonists or *katoikoi* in Ancient Greece and in the Hellenistic east.
Poliorcetica	The art of siege warfare.
Proteichisma	A stone slope built around a fortification, used to seal off any enemy tunnels and to keep battering rams away from the walls.
Rampart	A bank of earth, used for defence.
Stretchers	Ashlar stones laid in a wall.
Tetrapyrgion	Citadel or fortified palace characterized by four corner towers.

Index